Real Food, Real Good

Michael Smith
Real Food,
Eat Well with Over 100 of My Simple, Wholesome Recipes
Real Good

Photography by Ryan Szulc

PENGUIN

an imprint of Penguin Canada Books Inc., a division of Penguin Random House Canada Limited

Published by the Penguin Group

Penguin Canada Books Inc., 320 Front Street West, Suite 1400, Toronto, Ontario M5V 3B6, Canada

Penguin Group (USA) LLC, 375 Hudson Street, New York, New York 10014, U.S.A.
Penguin Books Ltd, 80 Strand, London WC2R 0RL, England
Penguin Ireland, 25 St Stephen's Green, Dublin 2, Ireland (a division of Penguin Books Ltd)
Penguin Group (Australia), 707 Collins Street, Melbourne, Victoria 3008, Australia
Penguin Books India Pvt Ltd, 11 Community Centre, Panchsheel Park, New Delhi – 110 017, India
Penguin Group (NZ), 67 Apollo Drive, Rosedale, Auckland 0632, New Zealand
Penguin Books (South Africa) (Pty) Ltd, 24 Sturdee Avenue, Rosebank, Johannesburg 2196, South Africa
Penguin Books Ltd, Registered Offices: 80 Strand, London WC2R 0RL, England

First published 2016

1 2 3 4 5 6 7 8 9 10

Copyright © Michael Smith, 2016
Food photography by Ryan Szulc
Food styling by Melanie Stuparyk
Prop styling by Catherine Doherty
Food production by Tiffany Tong

Manufactured in China

Library and Archives Canada Cataloguing in Publication

Smith, Michael, author
Real food, real good : eat well with over 100 of my simple, wholesome recipes /
Michael Smith.

ISBN 978-0-14-319219-0 (paperback)
ISBN 978-0-7352-3270-9 (eBook)

1. Cooking (Natural foods). 2. Cookbooks. I. Title.
TX714.S5993 2016   641.5'63   C2015-908746-5

www.penguinrandomhouse.ca

This book is dedicated to my family. To my delicious wife, Chazz,
my oyster-shucking teenager, Gabe, and firecracker daughters, Ariella and Camille.
Thank you. You guys are everything to me. I love loving the lot of ya!

Also By Michael Smith

Contents

The Real Food Pledge

Making healthy choices in the kitchen is essential for your best life. How you gather, prepare and share food profoundly affects who you are each and every day. The stakes are high. Society is struggling against a relentless hurricane of less and less home cooking, more and more nutritionally vacant processed food and the resulting health crisis. Don't fall prey. Protect your family. You can help choose your best life by choosing to cook real food. It may be unfamiliar turf but it's friendly territory. Just do your best, and I promise you'll enjoy the results!

I pledge to stand firm, to make informed choices and embrace simple home cooking as the best way to eliminate artificiality from my food and add the vibrancy of true health. I promise to share my table and serve as an example to my family and other cooks. I know a healthy food lifestyle is essential, accessible, easy, inexpensive and most of all delicious.

Chef Michael Smith

What Is Real Food?

- Real Food nourishes mind, body and soul.

- Real Food is ethically gathered from trusted sustainable producers.

- Real Food often gives the cook a personal connection to their raw ingredients through face-to-face local food connections.

- Real Food is prepared with time-honoured simplicity from natural, wholesome ingredients.

- Real Food does not need elaborate equipment, intricate methods or hours of labour. It's thoughtful and simple.

- Real Food is fun to cook. The path is pleasing and the journey delightful for all your senses.

- Real Food is made to be shared with family and friends, even hungry strangers and new friends.

- Real Food is deliberately and powerfully nutritious. It delivers the promise of a healthy life and vitality.

- Real Food is delicious and healthy because it connects peak flavour to peak nutrition.

- Real Food is light. It doesn't weigh you down with unbalanced calories and empty promises.

- Real Food respects the cook as much as it does the guests.

- Real Food is the antidote for highly processed food. With it you can rid your life of harmful additives and profit-driven processing.

- Real Food means eating anything you like. Just make it yourself and don't eat too much.

- Real Food always includes a homemade treat!

Real Food Strategies

You can fill your life with real food without embarking on a complicated mission. Just stick to the basics and forget all the fuss. So much of the battle is won with simple effort. In no time at all, you'll be a pro in the kitchen!

1. **BE DELIBERATE** Do you feel you need to change your nutritional routine? Does it feel daunting? Does that become an excuse for not changing? It may well be intimidating, but you can do it. The unknown always seems like a struggle at first, but, like so many things in life, once you get started, your new routines will soon become second nature. It will be hard work at first, but real effort just makes the results that much more satisfying.

2. **GET INSPIRED** I'm inspired by my kids to be the best I can be in the kitchen. They deserve to grow up healthy and full of energy, and my wife and I believe as parents it's our responsibility to ensure they do. Even if you're not a parent, there's inspiration all around us. You're preceded by and surrounded by legions of cooks that have successfully navigated their way through the very same changes. If they can do it, so can you!

3. **GET INFORMED** Information will motivate you. Don't allow indifference or ignorance to blind you to the realities of the food systems around you. Form your own opinions and make informed decisions. Look for impartial voices like the Center for Science in the Public Interest (CSPI) or authors like Michael Pollan.

4. **CLEAR YOUR SHELVES** One of the single most significant decisions you will ever make is to eliminate processed food from your diet. You may need to get radical and clear your shelves. Change your shopping habits. Don't let factories cook for you. Don't worry, you won't need much room for all the simplicity ahead.

5. **PLAN AHEAD** Spend time to save time. So much potential kitchen stress can be avoided by just organizing yourself. Do some meal planning, get rid of the guesswork, make a shopping list and set a regular time for shopping.

6. **MAKE AHEAD** We're all crunched for time, so there are lots of books, magazines and websites devoted to cooking meals in advance. You can join the legions of cooks that have discovered how easy it is to organize their routines this way. A weekend cooking rally easily sets you up for success in the week ahead!

7. **READ LABELS** Be informed. So many bad habits can easily be changed by simply arming yourself with the information that's right in front of you. If you need a nudge away from processed food, reading labels can really help. It's shocking how many empty promises, calories, chemicals, additives and forms of hidden salt and sugar are hiding in plain sight at your supermarket.

8. **BUY IN BULK** If you find yourself often returning to a particular ingredient, you may find it less expensive in the long run to buy it in bulk. You'll also appreciate the vast choice available in the bulk foods section or at your local bulk foods store.

9. **GO LOCAL** The best cooking is a celebration of the seasons. Become a regular at your favourite farmers' market. Try planting some vegetables in your backyard or growing a favourite vegetable or herb on a windowsill. Make an effort to learn about the harvest cycles and celebrate them. You'll never take a tomato for granted again after you spend a summer waiting for yours to ripen!

10. **GET CONNECTED** It's inspiring when you know the people who produce food for you. A real human connection with your ingredients can elevate them from commodities to treasures. Understanding the true work that goes into producing your food motivates your best cooking.

11. **START SMALL** Pick a day, pick a recipe and commit to cooking a real meal. You're not striving for perfection—you're just making a meal. Even if you struggle a bit, you're making progress. Share the results with your family and try not to worry about the outcome. It's just cooking, so experiment and have fun!

12. **SHARE THE LOAD** Invite your family or friends to give you a hand. You might enjoy preparing meals together, or you may just want help shopping, keeping your kitchen tidy or doing the dishes. Perhaps one or two nights a week, let someone else become your Chef at Home. Most families don't rely on one person to do everything in the kitchen.

13. **HAVE FUN** Do your very best to find the joy in cooking and eating. Sometimes we burden ourselves with unrealistic expectations that can lead to a sense of failure. Perhaps a weekend cooking session or two without the time pressures of the work week can help too. If you're finding the time to cook and share real food, then you've already achieved success. Pat yourself on the back. I love discovering a new dish and mastering it. You'll enjoy your food much more when you know it's real!

14. **SHARE A MEAL** One of life's great pleasures is sharing a real meal with your family. So much happens when we disconnect from our busy lives and connect with each other around the table. This is truly life at its best and may serve as the regular reminder you need to stay on track with your new Real Food lifestyle!

Superfoods for Your Kitchen

Some foods hit all the marks. They're packed with intense nutrition, loaded with big flavours and classic tastes, conveniently found in your local supermarket, affordable and easy to prepare. They're superfoods. And you don't need to be a nutritionist to enjoy them. Choose a great ingredient and just leave it at that. Even if you forget all the various macro- and micronutrients in your ingredients, they're still there!

- kale, spinach, broccoli and other dark green vegetables
- root vegetables
- sweet potatoes
- fruits and berries
- red bell peppers
- ancient grains
- legumes
- nuts
- quinoa and chia seeds
- yogurt
- eggs
- herbs and spices

Real Ingredients: Everything You Need

MEAT AND POULTRY

Beef • Lamb • Pork • Chicken • Duck • Turkey

Chosen wisely, meat is an excellent source of vital protein and minerals. But it can also contain high levels of fat and cholesterol, and some livestock is forced to endure shocking living conditions to keep costs down. The key is moderate consumption of ethically raised animals. Local sourcing can help you establish a trusted source. Processed sandwich meat and commercial sausages are often packed with harmful additives and should be avoided.

High-Quality Protein • Essential Amino Acids • Vitamins B_{12} & B_6 • Selenium • Phosphorus • Niacin • Choline • Riboflavin • Zinc

FRESH FISH AND SHELLFISH

Cod • Haddock • Hake • Halibut • Salmon • Trout • Clams • Mussels • Oysters • Crab • Shrimp • Lobster

A diet rich in fish is one of the smartest choices you can make. Fish and shellfish are nutrient dense and a particularly good source of the vital omega-3 essential fatty acids that contribute so mightily to good heart, brain and overall health. Oily fish such as salmon, mackerel, sardines and fresh tuna are your very best choices. Try to include them on your menu at least three times a week. Overfishing has depleted many wild fish stocks, so choose sustainable options from your supermarket or fishmonger.

High-Quality Protein • Essential Amino Acids • Vitamins • Minerals • Omega-3 Fatty Acids

BERRIES

Blackberries • Blueberries • Cranberries • Haskap • Strawberries • Raspberries

In nature, the very same molecules that contribute so much to the colour of fruit also contain powerful nutritional benefits. The micronutrient anthocyanin is concentrated in the purple of blackberries, blueberries and haskaps. Other antioxidants are equally strong in the red berries. Interestingly, as fruits ripen and their colours deepen, their micronutrients peak too. So the better the fruit tastes, the better it is for you!

High Calorie • Dietary Fibre • Vitamins • Minerals • Antioxidants • Flavonoids • Carotenoids • Phytonutrients • Anthocyanins

CITRUS FRUIT

Grapefruit • Lemons • Limes • Oranges

Lemons, limes and oranges are powerfully flavoured and protect against cardiovascular disease and various cancers. Oranges in particular are packed with vitamin C, one of the most powerful antioxidants. The skin of these fruits is loaded with intense aromatic flavour and more vital nutrients that can easily be included in your cooking by zesting. If you're a big OJ drinker, your best choice is to juice your fruit at home and so include as much of the fruit's natural metabolism-regulating fibre as possible.

Vitamin C • Fibre • Phytonutrients • Carotenoids • Flavonoids • Folates • Potassium • Calcium

TREE FRUIT

Apples • Apricots • Cherries • Peaches • Pears • Plums

Tree fruits are my favourite snack. They hit all the marks. A freshly picked, perfectly ripe fruit is loaded with addictive aromatic flavour, powerful sweetness and intense nutrition. These fruits are an amazing source of energy because they balance some of the highest sugar loads in nature with magical metabolism-slowing abilities. Mother Nature has blessed them with fibre and a suite of micronutrients that help the body absorb their natural sugars without harm.

High Calorie • Carbohydrates • High Dietary Fibre • Vitamins • Minerals • Antioxidants • Flavonoids • Phytonutrients • Anthocyanins

BANANAS AND TROPICAL FRUIT

Bananas • Guava • Lychee • Mangoes • Mangosteen • Papaya • Passion Fruit • Pineapples

Tropical fruits are among the most flavourful ingredients in the global pantry and stuffed with unique micronutrients. Like all fruits, they're great sources of sugar, thus high in energy. Bananas in particular are loaded with metabolism-regulating fibre and are a daily bedrock for my family. I pack four into our smoothie every single morning!

High Calorie • Carbohydrates • High Dietary Fibre • Vitamins • Minerals • Antioxidants • Flavonoids • Carotenoids • Phytonutrients

ORANGE JUICE

Juice it yourself

Ever noticed how different commercial orange juices taste from each other? Do you imagine a particularly lush and flavourful orange grove in the sun somewhere? Nope. It's a question of formulas, not varietals. Commercial orange juices are heavily processed, their flavours proprietary recipes designed in food labs. Unless you squeeze it yourself, orange juice is just flat pop. These liquid calories can be just as challenging for your body, no matter what the source. The key is moderation.

High Calorie • Carbohydrates • Vitamins • Minerals

FROZEN FRUIT

Blackberries • Blueberries • Cherries • Mangoes • Peaches • Pineapple • Raspberries • Strawberries

My family is fruit powered. We start every day with a fruit-filled smoothie. We all love the flavour and texture of frozen fruit, and I love the convenience and nutrition. Frozen fruit retains every bit of its micronutrient profile, and since it's harvested and frozen at peak ripeness it can actually have more nutrients than fresh fruit.

High Calorie • Carbohydrates • High Dietary Fibre • Vitamins • Minerals • Antioxidants • Flavonoids • Carotenoids • Phytonutrients

HEARTY GREENS

Chard • Collards • Kale • Spinach

Dark leafy greens are particularly tasty and healthy. They're some of the best ways for you to include lots of dark green nutrition in your cooking. The pigments in dark green vegetables are among the healthiest micronutrients. They're proven anti-inflammatory and antioxidant cancer fighters. Eat as many as you can, each and every day.

Fibre • Vitamins • Minerals • Antioxidants • Flavonoids • Carotenoids • Phytonutrients

BABY GREENS

Arugula • Chard • Kale • Spinach

One of my favourite ways of adding a big boost of dark green vegetable power to my cooking is with baby greens. They're a great addition to your favourite salads, soups or stews. Just stir them in at the last second to preserve their intense flavour and colour. They're tasty and convenient and found in most grocery stores.

Fibre • Vitamins • Minerals • Antioxidants • Flavonoids • Carotenoids • Phytonutrients

ASIAN GREENS

Bok Choy • Choy Sum • Gai Choy • Gai Lan • Pea Shoots • Yau Choy

This ubiquitous term refers to a wide variety of greens common to the various cuisines of southern and eastern Asia. They were once seen as exotic but are now mainstream enough to be grown commercially in greenhouses across Canada. It's no surprise that they're tasty and nutritious, but what I like best is how easy they make it to introduce to your family's table more healthy flavours from around the world.

Fibre • Vitamins • Minerals • Antioxidants • Flavonoids • Carotenoids • Phytonutrients

SQUASH

Acorn Squash • Butternut Squash • Spaghetti Squash • Marrow • Pumpkin • Zucchini

European explorers found many edible treasures in the new world, including the ubiquitous squash family. A favourite choice in the autumn, these vegetables are prized for their tasty nutritional intensity and artistic potential. Can you imagine Halloween without pumpkins? Nope. But I can imagine pumpkin pie without pumpkin, since the tastiest fillings are not made from jack-o'-lanterns, rather a sweeter, more flavourful variety.

Carbohydrates • High Dietary Fibre • Vitamins • Minerals • Antioxidants • Flavonoids • Carotenoids • Phytonutrients

ROOT VEGETABLES

Beets • Carrots • Celery Root • Parsnips • Rutabagas • Turnips

Plants tend to store the energy of the sunlight in their roots through the magic of photosynthesis, changing above-the-ground light into below-the-ground sugar. Root vegetables are packed with micronutrients. With a variety of rich, earthy flavours, this family of ingredients is one of the most valued in the pantry.

Carbohydrates • High Dietary Fibre • Vitamins • Minerals • Antioxidants • Flavonoids • Carotenoids • Phytonutrients

POTATOES

White-Fleshed • Red-Fleshed • Yellow-Fleshed • Baking • Boiling • High-Starch • Low-Starch

Cultures all over the world have found some particular local plant that yields a sweet, bland root ripe for easy cooking. Ours is the potato. It's a root vegetable, infinitely versatile, surprisingly nutritious and always tasty. Here on Prince Edward Island it reigns supreme, and the first baked potato of the year is always cause for celebration. Encourage your family to eat the skin: much of the fibre is concentrated there.

Carbohydrates • Dietary Fibre • Vitamins • Minerals • Antioxidants • Phytonutrients

SWEET POTATOES

Bright orange sweet potatoes are root vegetables just like their white potato cousins, but they're plainly more colourful and much sweeter. They're also packed with far more micronutrients. No surprise. In nature the very same molecules that contribute to colour and flavour also contain powerful nutritional benefits. But what about the butter? Your body needs a bit of fat to best absorb the high levels of beta-carotene that give sweet potatoes their characteristic bright orange intensity. When was the last time *adding* butter made something healthier?

Carbohydrates • High Dietary Fibre • Vitamins • Minerals • Antioxidants • Flavonoids • Carotenoids • Phytonutrients • Anthocyanins

BRASSICAS

Broccoli • Brussels Sprouts • Cabbages • Cauliflower • Kohlrabi • Rapini

These vegetables are some of the most widely grown in the world. They're nutritionally dense, packed with vitamin C and loaded with fibre and a wide variety of micronutrients and phytochemicals. They're also universally tasty, largely because their slight, pleasing bitterness is balanced by their inherent sweetness and bold flavour. Diets that include lots of brassicas closely correlate with lower incidences of cancer.

Fibre • Vitamins • Minerals • Antioxidants • Flavonoids • Carotenoids • Phytonutrients

ONIONS AND GARLIC

Yellow Onions • White Onions • Red Onions • Sweet Onions • Garlic

I couldn't imagine cooking without these two key ingredients. All over the world they form part of the aromatic flavour base for dish after dish. They're distinctive enough to give character to your cooking but neutral enough to welcome lots of other aromatic ingredients. The sweetness of onions allows them to brown easily and add yet another dimension of flavour. Both are packed with various micronutrients that are closely associated with their intense flavour. Delicious and good for you!

Vitamins • Minerals • Antioxidants • Flavonoids • Carotenoids • Phytonutrients

GREEN ONIONS

Green Onions (Scallions) • Spring Onions • Chives

Green onions are one of my all-time favourite ingredients, although nutritionally speaking there's little difference between green and white onions. They're an easy and convenient way to add a big boost of last-second flavour to lots of dishes. The key is their mildness: you can eat them raw. Thinly sliced, they add a wonderful herbaceous sharpness and gorgeous burst of green to a wide range of dishes.

Vitamins • Minerals • Antioxidants • Flavonoids • Carotenoids • Phytonutrients

FROZEN VEGETABLES

Broccoli • Brussels Sprouts • Carrots • Cauliflower • Corn • Kale • Peas • Spinach

We'd all love to live next to a beautiful garden full of miraculously year-round, ever-bearing vegetables. The next best thing is a freezer. Modern freezing methods lock in nutrients. Frozen vegetables are an excellent alternative to fresh and far surpass canned versions in quality and taste. I also love the convenient boost of colour and flavour they add to so many soups and stews.

Fibre • Vitamins • Minerals • Antioxidants • Flavonoids • Carotenoids • Phytonutrients

CANNED TOMATOES

Whole • Chopped • Diced • Puréed • Crushed • Paste

Fresh supermarket tomatoes can be under-ripe and bland. That lack of flavour means nutrient levels are also low. Raw tomatoes are also missing a key micronutrient. Canned tomatoes ripen on the vine, so they're picked at peak nutrition. Their sunny flavours are locked into the can as fast and fresh as possible. The processing heat is enough to release the powerful cancer-fighting micronutrient lycopene. Watch how much sodium is added to the can, though. Choose lower-salt options.

Fibre • Vitamins • Minerals • Antioxidants • Flavonoids • Carotenoids • Phytonutrients

FRESH HERBS

Basil • Bay • Cilantro • Dill • Lovage • Marjoram • Mint • Oregano • Parsley •
Rosemary • Sage • Savory • Tarragon • Thyme

In nature, flavour intensity often matches more than just nutritional strength.
These powerfully flavoured herbs were once harvested for their medicinal
properties too. Today we value them for their flavour, but they're still packed
with phytonutrients. They're a wonderful way to perfume your cooking with
bright, aromatic personality and maybe even a little preventative medicine.

Antibacterial • Anti-inflammatory • Flavonoids • Micronutrients • Phytonutrients

DRIED HERBS

Basil • Bay • Cilantro • Dill • Lovage • Marjoram • Mint • Oregano • Parsley •
Rosemary • Sage • Savory • Tarragon • Thyme

The heightened flavours and nutrients in herbs are largely concentrated in
various volatile oils that survive drying. The many and varied flavours of dried
herbs season a myriad of dishes. A little bit always goes a long way because
they're much more pungent than their fresh counterparts. These herbs are
often interchangeable, so try improvising with them. Respect tradition but
don't feel bound by it. Store in a cool, dark place.

Antibacterial • Anti-inflammatory • Flavonoids • Micronutrients • Phytonutrients

SPICES

Allspice • Caraway • Cardamom • Chili • Cinnamon • Cloves • Coriander • Cumin •
Curry • Fennel • Juniper • Star Anise • Mace • Nutmeg • Paprika • Saffron •
Turmeric • Vanilla

Whereas herbs are leaves, spices come from every other part of the plant:
seeds, fruits, roots, bark, berries, buds. As with herbs, spices were first discovered by medicine seekers but are now valued for flavour. Spices offer cooks a
connection to time and place and a journey as compelling as the destination.
They can be haunting and mysterious or bright and bold. The choice is yours.

Antibacterial • Anti-inflammatory • Flavonoids • Phytonutrients

SEA SALT

Coarse • Fine • Kosher • Non-iodized • Pickling

All salt comes from the sea. Ancient oceans left deposits of our only edible rock
all over the globe. It's indispensable in the kitchen, a valuable preservative and
vital for life. In moderation it helps regulate our metabolism. Lightly seasoned
home cooking includes plenty of salt for both flavour and nutritive value. Don't
let Big Food Inc. lure you with your instinctive love of salt's savoury taste, though.
They overload their products with way too much to mask the inadequacy of
processed flavour. One more reason to stay away from processed food.

Minerals

GINGER

This powerful root is blessed with two strengths: it's intensely aromatic and wildly healthy. Its flavours and benefits are so strong that in many cultures it's considered a medicine. Fresh ginger is tasty, but you have to use it quickly. Dried ginger is aromatic but not quite as intense. A handy trick to preserve fresh ginger: stick it in your freezer. When it's rock hard it's easily grated into an intensely flavoured powder that retains its sharp freshness.

Antibacterial • Anti-inflammatory • Flavonoids • Micronutrients • Phytonutrients

MUSTARD

Ballpark • Brown • Dijon • Grainy • Honey • Yellow

Mustard is one of the most widely used condiments in the world, and Canada grows more of it than any other country. Its sharp pungency lends aromatic complexity to many a dish. It's also the secret ingredient in my homemade vinaigrettes because of its emulsifying abilities. Mustard contains lecithin, which helps bring water and oil together into smooth salad dressings.

Vitamins • Minerals • Phytonutrients

HOT PEPPERS AND HOT SAUCES

Chili Peppers • Peppercorns • Sriracha Sauce

Controlled spicy heat is one of the great joys of eating. The volatile oils responsible are powerful protection for their plants and equally stimulating for your palate. Spicy heat wakes up your taste buds, allowing you to taste more of the other flavours present than you might otherwise perceive. Because real pain can be involved, though, your brain triggers counteracting endorphins that leave you feeling euphoric. That heat is best enjoyed in moderation, with lots of aromatic flavour. That's why Sriracha is my favourite hot sauce. It's spicy enough to boost your taste buds, but not spicy enough to overwhelm them.

Antibacterial • Anti-inflammatory • Flavonoids • Phytonutrients

OLIVE OIL

Extra-Virgin • First Cold Pressed

Olive oil is my favourite oil because it's very healthy and wonderfully aromatic. The very best oils can be fruity, flowery, even peppery and always insanely tasty. They're also heart-healthy and help balance cholesterol levels. Some oils are pale imitations, though. The key is to buy minimally processed oil from a trusted source. Heat destroys much of the flavour that makes olive oil distinctive, so for cooking, use a less expensive (but still good-quality) oil, and save your expensive one for things like salad dressings.

Micronutrients • Antioxidants • Anti-inflammatory • Flavonoids • Phytonutrients • Vitamin E

VEGETABLE OILS

Canola • Coconut • Corn • Grapeseed • Peanut • Safflower • Soybean • Sunflower

When vegetable oils are heated they can degrade and release high levels of potentially harmful agents that should be avoided. In general, all these oils are okay for unheated uses, bland but generally harmless, none better than aromatic olive. Start frying and sautéing, though, and some degrade quickly from the heating. Canola and more expensive olive are great choices, while coconut is particularly stable and a good choice for general-purpose cooking too.

Micronutrients • Antioxidants • Anti-inflammatory • Flavonoids • Phytonutrients • Vitamin E

BUTTER AND LARD

Good old-fashioned animal fats have been demonized for far too long. As the evils of processing and heating vegetable oils have become more understood, these once ignored fats have been rediscovered and are now being lauded for their wholesomeness—not surprising, considering that butter originates from animals, not factories, while lard adds incomparable texture and crispness to pastry. This isn't permission to go crazy (as with all things, the key remains moderation). It's just recognition that Mother Nature was right all along.

High Calorie • Saturated Fat • Cholesterol

VINEGARS

Red Wine • White Wine • Rice Wine • Balsamic • Cider

Vinegar has some nutritional benefits, but its main role in the kitchen is to add pleasing or balancing sourness. It's an essential preservative for pickling too. More than anything else, I use it in vinaigrettes. Keeping a bottle or two on the shelf means you're always prepped to mix together your own salad dressings. Vinegars are mostly interchangeable, so feel free to substitute one for the other and experiment a bit.

Antioxidants • Phytonutrients

HONEY

Buckwheat • Clover • Wildflower • Blended • Monofloral • Polyfloral

Honey is perhaps the most concentrated form of naturally occurring sugar in nature. Various types offer some health benefits, but none that outweigh the simple fact that you're largely consuming pure sugar. You may prefer honey's aromatic flavour and more natural origins over factory-made white and brown sugars, but high concentrations of sugar can overwhelm your body's metabolism no matter where they come from.

High Calorie • Carbohydrates

MAPLE SYRUP

Maple syrup is my favourite sweetener. It's produced by reducing the spring sap of a maple tree by 40:1 into a syrup. I love its Canadian roots, earthy flavour and tradition. It contains a much higher level of micronutrients than plain white sugar, which makes it an excellent sweetener choice, but it's still sugar, and too much of any sugar will overwhelm your metabolism. I prefer darker grades of maple syrup, as they have more flavour and antioxidants.

Trace Vitamins • Minerals • Antioxidants

100% WHOLE WHEAT FLOUR (WITH NO ADDED FLOURS)

Whole wheat grains are seeds and thus they have three parts: high-fibre bran on the outside to protect the seed's energy source on the inside, the micronutrient-rich germ and carb-heavy endosperm. Most of the time the bran and germ are removed so the remaining bland white endosperm can become gluten-rich yet nutritionally poor white flour. True whole wheat flour retains all three parts and provides you with a source of incredibly balanced rich nutrition. No surprise, it tastes better too!

Protein • Essential Amino Acids • Carbohydrates • High Dietary Fibre • Vitamins • Minerals • Antioxidants • Phytonutrients

DRIED PASTA

Cannelloni • Farfalle • Fettuccine • Fusilli • Gemelli • Linguine • Orecchiette • Pappardelle • Penne • Rotini • Spaghetti • Tagliatelle

The many and varied forms of pasta are an excellent pantry staple. They offer an easy path to a simple meal with a nearly limitless variety of dishes. They're a perfectly acceptable source of carbohydrates, and provide essential energy. They're best cooked al dente—tender enough to bite but firm enough to stay pleasingly chewy. Whole wheat pasta is often a refined non-whole-grain product. Try to avoid serving any pasta with rich, creamy sauces. The added fat can tip pasta into the danger zone.

Carbohydrates • Protein • Gluten • Vitamins • Minerals

BROWN RICE

Rice is the seed of a grass plant. In its many forms it is, perhaps, the world's most important staple food, accounting for more than 20 percent of our collective daily global calorie intake. Rice powers the planet. It's also a good source of micronutrients. To maximize its fibre load, choose brown varieties. They retain the rice seed's protective coating, the fibre-rich bran.

High-Quality Protein • Gluten-Free • Essential Amino Acids • Complex Carbohydrates • High Dietary Fibre • Vitamins • Minerals

ANCIENT GRAINS

Amaranth • Barley • Buckwheat • Bulgur • Farro • Kamut • Maize • Millet • Oats •
Rye • Spelt

We evolved with ancient grains at the core of our diet. We can't keep pace with
modern processing, though. Modern wheat, corn and rice are the product of
genetic manipulation that unfortunately lessens their once higher nutritive
value. Ancient grains are celebrated for retaining their original balanced and
often vastly superior nutritional profiles.

*Protein • Essential Amino Acids • Carbohydrates • High Dietary Fibre • Vitamins •
Minerals • Antioxidants • Phytonutrients*

QUINOA AND CHIA

Quinoa and chia seeds don't come from grass plants, so they're not whole
grains. They're tasty, though, and they're cooked in much the same way as
whole grains, but they go one better: these seeds are superfoods. Ounce for
ounce they're intensely nutritious. They pack a full protein profile and are
loaded with a laundry list of micronutrients. They're also inexpensive. Need
any more convincing?

*Protein • Gluten-Free • Essential Amino Acids • Carbohydrates • High Dietary Fibre •
Vitamins • Minerals • Antioxidants • Phytonutrients*

PULSES AND LEGUMES

Adzuki Beans • Black-Eyed Peas • Chickpeas (Garbanzo Beans) • Kidney Beans •
Lentils • Lima Beans • Mung Beans • Navy Beans • Pinto Beans • Red Beans •
Split Peas

Pulses and legumes are seeds, so they contain all the elements for new life in a
perfect tiny package. It's no surprise that those very same nutrients are excellent
for fuelling human life too, particularly fibre, which regulates blood sugar
levels and protein. They're a much better source of sustainable protein than an
environmentally draining meat-heavy diet. Maybe that's why pulses and legumes
are the primary source of protein for billions of people every single day.

*High-Quality Protein • Gluten-Free • Essential Amino Acids • Complex Carbohydrates •
High Dietary Fibre • Vitamins • Minerals*

CANNED BEANS

Black • Chickpeas (Garbanzo Beans) • Great Northern • Kidney • Navy • Pinto •
Red • White

Ounce for ounce, beans' balance of fibre and protein makes them one of the
world's healthiest foods. Canned beans are a convenient way to add these
nutrients to your diet. They're not affected by the canning process, so their
nutrition is not lost when you rinse the beans. You can take the time to soak
and cook them from raw, but if you're short on time, it's way easier to just
open up a can.

Protein • Essential Amino Acids • High Dietary Fibre • Vitamins • Minerals

NUTS

Almonds • Brazil • Cashews • Chestnuts • Hazelnuts • Macadamia • Peanuts • Pecans • Pistachios • Pine Nuts • Walnuts

The world is full of nuts. Their hard shells are yet another way Mother Nature protects her vital seeds. Within their strong coating is everything a tree needs to grow: lots of micronutrients and an excellent source of energy. Tasty energy—nuts are packed with delicious oils. Turns out what's good for trees is good for humans too. Maybe that's why I like hugging them!

Protein • Gluten-Free • High Unsaturated Fat • Essential Amino Acids • High Calorie • High Dietary Fibre • Vitamins • Minerals • Antioxidants • Phytonutrients

NUT BUTTERS

Almond • Cashew • Hazelnut • Macadamia • Peanut

Nuts are easily ground into a smooth, delicious paste that's perfect for a nutritionally dense snack or for adding to your cooking. Watch out for commercial brands, though. Processors often ruin this all-natural ingredient with added sugar and emulsifiers. It's normal for the healthy oil in nut butters to separate—just stir it back in.

Protein • Gluten-Free • High Unsaturated Fat • Essential Amino Acids • High Calorie • High Dietary Fibre • Vitamins • Minerals • Antioxidants • Phytonutrients

MILK

Whole • 2% • Skim

Drinking and cooking with milk is an easy and excellent way to get a big boost of energy with a strong shot of protein, vitamins and minerals. Just be sure your cows were happy, though. In Canada (unlike our neighbour to the south), growth hormones and steroids cannot be given to dairy cows, and antibiotics cannot be present in dairy that's for sale. There can also be concerns regarding the inhumane treatment of dairy cows, so best to ask questions or buy organic when you can.

High-Quality Protein • High Calorie • Carbohydrates • Vitamins • Minerals

YOGURT

Full-Fat • Greek • Plain (no flavours, real or otherwise) • No additives • No sugar

The world loves yogurt. More milk is used to make yogurt than is drunk plain. For eons the light bacterial fermentation of milk has been an efficient path to enhanced nutrition. Today, though, commercial yogurt is often corrupted with sugar, additives and thickeners. Stay away. Stick to the most plain, basic type and you'll enjoy the same nutrition that has characterized yogurt for centuries.

High-Quality Protein • High Calorie • Carbohydrates • Vitamins • Minerals

CHEESE
Cow • Goat • Sheep

Dairy farmers discovered long ago that the most efficient way to preserve the rich nutrients of their herds' raw milk is to make cheese. Milk can be naturally fermented in many ways—crème fraîche, sour cream, buttermilk, yogurt, kefir—but cheese curds can be the most concentrated and, with care, the most valuable. Enjoy the award-winning cheeses of Canada and the world, and as always avoid processed versions.

High-Quality Protein • High Calorie • Carbohydrates • Vitamins • Minerals

EGGS
Chicken • Duck • Brown • White

Mother Nature creates an egg as a tidy little package of enough micro- and macronutrients to sustain a new life. It's no wonder they're so powerfully nutritious. They're packed with enough protein to kick meat off the menu and they're easily cooked in many delicious ways.

High-Quality Protein • Essential Amino Acids • Vitamins • Minerals • Calories • Fat

MILK SUBSTITUTES
Almond (homemade) • Rice • Soy

Many consumers prefer to avoid lactose and, in the U.S., the rampant hormones and antibiotics in commercial milk. They still crave the concentrated liquid nutrition, though. Milk substitutes can be a viable alternative unless they're over-processed. Avoid additives, sweeteners and thickeners. Commercial nut milks are laughably devoid of actual nuts and should be avoided, but you can make your own at home.

High-Quality Protein • Essential Amino Acids • High Calorie • Carbohydrates • High Dietary Fibre • Vitamins • Minerals • Antioxidants • Flavonoids • Carotenoids • Phytonutrients

COCONUT
Cream • Milk • Oil • Water

Coconut water is the liquid harvested from young, often immature coconuts. Coconut milk is made by grating mature coconuts and dissolving their fat through grinding and mixing with water. Coconut cream is the thick rich part that often floats to the top of the milk; you'll find it when you open an unshaken can. Coconut oil is derived from the cream and has many positive attributes. When buying coconut milk, look for brands that don't contain artificial emulsifiers, thickeners or sweeteners.

High Saturated Fat • Vitamins • Minerals • Antibacterial

WATER

Tap • Well • Still • Sparkling • Rushing Wild Mountain Stream

Even though plain old water is devoid of nutrients, it's still the single most important thing that we consume every single day. Drink lots. There are many variables—age and activity level among them—but we need to consume 1 to 2 quarts or litres a day to stay hydrated and healthy. Don't believe the hype, either: there's nothing wrong with good old-fashioned tap water. Bottled water is just an expensive convenience.

Trace Minerals

POPCORN

Homemade popcorn is an excellent snack, and so simple to make. It offers lots of whole-grain goodness, complex carbohydrates and fibre without a big load of calories. It's convenient, inexpensive and wildly fun too. Every kid deserves to grow up watching a popping pot of the stuff go wild. Of course, go easy on the added fat, salt and sugar. Avoid the prepackaged stuff too. Its artificial flavours are a toxic reminder that factories can screw up even the simplest treat.

Carbohydrates • High Dietary Fibre • Vitamins • Minerals

DARK CHOCOLATE

There are many varieties of chocolate, many of them packed with artificial ingredients and flavours. White and milk chocolates often contain very little real chocolate and lots of sugar and harmful fats, so read the label! Dark chocolate with at least 70% cacao solids and fats is your best choice. It does contain some micronutrients but not enough to be significant. No matter how good the chocolate, it will always be a high-energy food—a.k.a. a treat.

High Calorie • Vitamins • Minerals • Antioxidants • Flavonoids

Watch List:
Read the Label

It's usually best to buy food that isn't prepackaged, but sometimes it can be your best choice. Be careful, though. Food labelling laws are heavily influenced by Big Food Inc., who bring to the table far more lawyers than nutritionists. Your best defence? Don't trust claims made on the front of the package. Read the label on the back. Look for disguised sugars and long strings of chemical names. Remember: if the product has a label at all, that means it's in a package, so be sure you've exhausted any fresher options.

Here are some terms and ingredients to be particularly skeptical of:

HEALTHY INGREDIENTS Many packaged foods contain just enough of an ingredient to allow it to be touted on the label but not enough to truly make it healthy. Trendy superfoods are easily manipulated to add a bit of marketing allure to foods that are otherwise devoid of nutrition.

NATURAL This claim is regulated in some aisles of the supermarket but ignored in most others. It has a very specific meaning in the meat department but is essentially meaningless elsewhere, especially on packaged food, where it can basically apply to anything, even heavily hydrogenated oil and high-fructose corn syrup.

SERVING SIZES One of the most popular tricks for high-fat, high-sugar and high-salt products is to reduce their serving size until their vital numbers fall into a "good" range. The problem is, the serving sizes are unrealistic. Who drinks half a can of pop?

FREE-RANGE You may believe these are the chickens living in pastoral splendour, roaming a vast farmer's field out in the country somewhere. Not so fast. This loosely interpreted term usually just means there's a door in a cage leading to a small outside pen overlooking the parking lot.

GLUTEN-FREE A small percentage of Canadians suffer from celiac disease, a rare autoimmune disorder triggered by gluten, a naturally occurring protein in wheat. It's a serious disease that deserves respect, but producers have hijacked it with boldly labelled products that don't contain gluten anyway but now somehow seem healthier.

NO ADDED SUGAR This doesn't mean that a product is sugar-free; it just means that sugar wasn't added. Fruit products often use this claim even though they're packed with naturally occurring (but artificially manipulated, very high) sugar levels.

MULTIGRAIN OR WHOLE GRAIN These terms are intentionally meant to evoke "100% whole grain" but are essentially meaningless. Manufacturers shape consumers' perceptions with minimal compliance. Did you know that using two different types of bland white flour qualifies something as "multi-grain"? Or that adding just a little bit of whole grain can mean the same pale white flours can be labelled "whole grain"? Your only assurance is to look for "100% whole grain."

FRUIT JUICE Fruits enjoy a well-deserved healthy aura—until you remove their metabolism-slowing fibre and squeeze out just another high-calorie liquid—sugary liquids masquerading behind exotic promises, including ethically dubious bare-minimum amounts of nutrition. Watch for the word "cocktail," which means added sugar. Apple juice concentrate may be the worst offender—it's basically pure sugar. So-called natural fruit apple juice is so overly processed that it's essentially refined to pure sugar, then diluted with water. Worse yet, Big Food Inc. is somehow still allowed to legally call the resultant liquid "apple juice."

So-Called Foods

Just because it's sold at your supermarket behind a bright, shiny label and you can put it in your mouth doesn't mean it deserves to be called food. Food-processing companies always look for the easiest way to manipulate the cheapest ingredients with even cheaper additives. Legions of food scientists do their best to trick your palate with addictive, fabricated flavours and not much else. Ease of shipping and shelf stability rank well above nutrition. These goods can be harmful, so buyer beware.

BREAKFAST CEREAL Sugar-laden breakfast cereals are simply breakfast candy. They're the worst way to start your day because what goes up must come down. Heading out the door on a sugar high sets you up for an inevitable crash later that morning.

PREMADE SAUCES AND DRESSINGS These salt and sugar bombs are stirred together with a laundry list of chemical additives and artificial thickeners. Ever wonder why there always seems to be a "stabilizer" somewhere on the label?

BOUILLON CUBES AND INSTANT GRAVY POWDERS Ever wonder how one little cube or spoonful of suspicious powder can flavour a potful of sauce? It can't! Not without a ton of salt and a whole lot of artificial flavour.

PRE-GRATED PARMESAN CHEESE If it doesn't need to be refrigerated, smells weird and looks like dusty powder in a can, is it really cheese? Not in my kitchen, and I wouldn't recommend it in yours.

HIGH-FRUCTOSE CORN SYRUP This highly refined liquid sugar is preferred by food processors because it's cheap. It's also one of the worst culprits in our global obesity epidemic, but frankly, no worse than any other sugar. The real issue remains not what type of sugar we consume but how much.

MARGARINE Mother Nature makes deliciously natural butter. Factories pump hydrogen gas into vegetable oil to make margarine. In my home, the choice between the two is simple.

CAKE MIXES AND FROSTINGS Quite possibly the most fake, additive-laden, preservative-protected (not that any smart bacteria would eat this stuff), sugar-heavy artificiality in supermarkets. Ever wonder how things like this can sit at room temperature for years without changing? It's not real!

BACON BITS Do yourself a favour. If a product is brazenly phony, don't touch it. It's not food. It's a science experiment and you're the guinea pig. Bacon bits are devoid of real meat. They're trumped up with fillers and phony flavours. Stay away.

"REAL" JUICE If a food processor feels compelled to call something "real," chances are it isn't. Bottled lemon and lime juice is loaded with harmful preservatives and heavily manipulated into a foul-tasting pale substitute for the real thing.

CHOCOLATE MILK The positive benefits of whole milk are ruined by a massive overdose of sugar and cheap artificial flavour. This should not be a daily staple but rather a treat now and then.

SODA POP The single worst way you can consume calories. It's liquid sugar immediately processed into body fat by your hard-working, over-stressed liver. Why push your body to the edge of a system breakdown? Drink water instead. The effects of soda pop on your body just aren't worth it.

20 Real Foods You Can Make at Home

Convenience has led us to forget that many everyday foods were once made at home. Most of these we now take for granted as supermarket staples, while others we seem to automatically regard as restaurant standbys. In fact, they can be whipped up easily in your kitchen, where you control what goes into your food.

1. **Bread** (page 221)
2. **Sausage** (page 51)
3. **Chicken broth** (see page 69)
4. **Beef broth** (page 243)
5. **Granola** (see page 40)
6. **Sour cream/crème fraîche** (page 250)
7. **Ketchup** (page 244)
8. **Mustard** (page 247)
9. **Salad dressings** (see pages 91–108)
10. **Barbecue sauce** (page 248)
11. **Fruit roll-ups** (page 55)
12. **Cookies** (pages 52 and 225)
13. **Marshmallows** (page 238)
14. **Caesar salad** (page 91)
15. **Hummus** (page 57)
16. **Sushi** (page 64)
17. **Gravy** (see page 131)
18. **Chicken wings** (page 119)
19. **Hand pies** (page 125)
20. **French fries** (page 206)

A Good Breakfast
and a Few Snacks

Raspberry Mango Mint Smoothie

I kick off every single day by whipping up a smoothie for my kids and packing it with enough nutritional density to keep them going all morning long. You can too. The key is to add enough flavour that they race to the bottom of the glass! This version is one of our favourites. It includes enough chia seed to add a real boost of omega-3 but not so much that it turns off your kids.

SERVES 4

1 cup (250 mL) of real yogurt
2 ripe bananas
2 cups (500 mL) of frozen mango chunks
1 cup (250 mL) of frozen raspberries

¼ cup (60 mL) of chia seeds
4 dates, pitted
3 whole sprigs of fresh mint
2 cups (500 mL) of orange juice

Pile everything into your blender in the order given and purée until smooth.

Oatmeal Pancakes with Bacon Maple Syrup

These have been my family's go-to pancakes for many years, but only recently have I taken them to the next level by serving them with bacon-infused maple syrup. Just when I thought they couldn't get any better, I proved myself wrong! **SERVES 4 TO 6**

For the bacon maple syrup
4 thick slices of bacon, thinly sliced crosswise
1 cup (250 mL) of pure maple syrup

For the pancakes
2 cups (500 mL) of whole wheat flour
1 cup (250 mL) of quick-cooking oats
2 tablespoons (30 mL) of baking powder
1 teaspoon (5 mL) of nutmeg
½ teaspoon (2 mL) of salt
2 eggs
2 cups (500 mL) of milk
2 tablespoons (30 mL) of coconut oil, vegetable oil or melted butter, plus more for cooking
2 tablespoons (30 mL) of honey
1 tablespoon (15 mL) of pure vanilla extract

Start by making the syrup. Toss the bacon into a heavy skillet over medium-high heat. Add a splash of water to help it cook evenly. Cook, stirring frequently, until the water has evaporated and the bacon is deliciously browned and evenly crisp, 10 minutes or so. Pour off some, most or none of the bacon fat. Pour in the maple syrup and bring to a slow, steady simmer. Bubble away as the syrup absorbs the flavour of the bacon and smoothly combines with the bacon fat, just a minute or two. Remove from the heat.

Make the pancakes. Heat your largest, heaviest skillet or griddle over medium to medium-low heat.

In a large bowl, whisk together the whole wheat flour, oats, baking powder, nutmeg and salt. In a second bowl, with the same whisk, mix together the eggs, milk, oil, honey and vanilla. Add the wet ingredients to the dry, switch to a wooden spoon and with just a few quick strokes stir until a smooth batter forms.

Lightly coat the skillet with a splash of oil. Spoon in the batter, making pancakes any size or shape you want. Cook until the bottoms are golden brown and firm. Flip and continue cooking until the second side is also golden brown. Serve with lots of bacon maple syrup.

Oatmeal-Crusted French Toast with Honey-Glazed Peaches

Looking for a special breakfast? Delicious French toast is an easy and impressive way to start your day, especially when it's topped with a fresh fruit compote. This recipe features an added crunchy bonus: a whole-grain crust on every slice. All you have to do is dip the works in rolled oats before you toast them in the pan. Whole-grain goodness in every bite! **SERVES 4**

For the peaches
2 tablespoons (30 mL) of butter
4 cups (1 L) of fresh or frozen peaches, cut into bite-size chunks
¼ cup (60 mL) of honey
1 tablespoon (15 mL) of pure vanilla extract
The zest and juice of 1 lemon

For the French toast
4 eggs
1 cup (250 mL) of milk
¼ cup (60 mL) of maple syrup
1 tablespoon (15 mL) of pure vanilla extract
1 teaspoon (5 mL) of nutmeg or cinnamon
8 slices of multigrain bread
1 cup (250 mL) of oat, spelt, rye or kamut flakes
2 tablespoons (30 mL) of vegetable oil
2 tablespoons (30 mL) of butter

Begin with the peaches. Melt the butter in a large sauté pan over medium heat. Add the peaches and cook just long enough to warm them through. Add the honey, vanilla and lemon zest and juice. Continue cooking and stirring until evenly glazed, just a minute or two longer. Remove from the heat and keep warm.

For the French toast, crack the eggs into a large bowl and whisk in the milk, maple syrup, vanilla and nutmeg. Arrange the bread slices in a single layer in a large shallow baking dish. Pour the egg mixture over them. Let sit, turning once or twice, until most of the egg mixture is absorbed, 5 minutes or so. Meanwhile, heat your largest, heaviest skillet or griddle over medium-low heat. Pour the whole-grain flakes into a shallow dish or plate.

Pour a small puddle of the oil into the hot pan and add a bit of the butter. Swirl until sizzling, adding the butter's flavour without burning it. One by one, dredge the slices of bread in the whole-grain flakes, turning to evenly coat each side and pressing gently to ensure the flakes adhere. Add as many bread slices to the pan as you can fit. Cook until the bottoms are golden brown and crisp, 3 or 4 minutes. Flip with a flourish and continue to cook until the second side is equally golden brown, a few minutes more. Repeat with the remaining oil, butter and bread slices. If you're expecting a crowd, you can hold the cooked ones in a 200°F (100°C) oven while you finish cooking the rest. Serve with the warm peaches.

Ancient Grain Granola Parfaits with Maple Blueberries and Yogurt

Few things are as satisfying as a bowl of wholesome granola, especially when you've made it yourself. Give it a shot. You'll quickly discover how easy it is to bake a batch and stir in a few of your own ideas. You'll be poised for lots of A.M. energy with this whole-grain goodness. Take it to the next level with a layer of maple blueberries in a classic parfait! **SERVES 8**

For the granola syrup
½ cup (125 mL) of vegetable oil
½ cup (125 mL) of maple syrup
¼ cup (60 mL) of brown sugar
1 tablespoon (15 mL) of pure vanilla extract
1 teaspoon (5 mL) of cinnamon
¼ teaspoon (1 mL) of freshly grated nutmeg
⅛ teaspoon (0.5 mL) of salt

For the granola
2 cups (500 mL) of large-flake rolled oats
½ cup (125 mL) of spelt flakes
½ cup (125 mL) of kamut flakes
½ cup (125 mL) of quinoa flakes
½ cup (125 mL) of soy flakes
½ cup (125 mL) of amaranth

½ cup (125 mL) of millet
¼ cup (60 mL) of chia seeds
¼ cup (60 mL) of freshly ground flaxseeds
2 cups (500 mL) or so of your favourite chopped nuts
2 cups (500 mL) or so of your favourite chopped dried fruit

For the blueberry compote
1 tablespoon (15 mL) of cornstarch
The zest and juice of 1 lemon
2 cups (500 mL) of frozen blueberries
½ cup (125 mL) of maple syrup

For the parfaits
Plain yogurt

Preheat your oven to 325°F (160°C). Turn on your convection fan if you have one. Line a baking sheet with parchment paper or a silicone baking mat.

To make the granola syrup, in a medium bowl, whisk together the oil, maple syrup, brown sugar, vanilla, cinnamon, nutmeg and salt. To make the granola, in a large bowl, whisk together the oats, spelt, kamut, quinoa, soy, amaranth, millet, chia seeds, flaxseeds and nuts. Pour the syrup over the grain mixture and stir until evenly coated.

Spread the granola evenly on the baking sheet. If you prefer loose granola, leave as is. If you prefer larger, chunkier pieces, press the works firmly with a spatula or the back of another baking sheet. Bake (stirring once or twice if you like finer pieces) until lightly browned and fragrant, 45 minutes or so. Cool completely on the baking sheet before breaking up into bite-size pieces or crumbling further into finer pieces. Toss in the dried fruit.

Meanwhile, make the blueberry compote. Stir the cornstarch into the lemon juice until dissolved. Stir the cornstarch mixture, lemon zest, blueberries and maple syrup together in a small pot and bring to a simmer over medium-high heat. Cook, stirring frequently, until thickened. Remove from the heat and cool.

To assemble the parfaits, spoon a thick layer of yogurt into clear jars or glasses. Generously top with layers of blueberry compote and granola. For travel-friendly treats, ¼ cup (60 mL) of yogurt, 2 tablespoons (30 mL) of compote and 2 tablespoons (30 mL) of granola fit perfectly into a ½-cup (125 mL) mason jar. For a more substantial meal, double these amounts into a wide-mouth 1-cup (250 mL) mason jar.

Ancient Grain Porridge with Cardamom Honey Pears

There's nothing like the sustained energy you receive from a bowl of whole-grain porridge. There's no better way to start your day. Not only will you enjoy lots of hearty, satisfying flavour but you'll also feel charged and energized for hours to come. Because these grains are not highly processed, your body takes its time slowly absorbing their nutrients and patiently rewarding you with lots of get-up-and-go! **SERVES 4**

For the porridge
4 cups (1 L) of water or milk
2 tablespoons (30 mL) of honey
¼ cup (60 mL) of steel-cut oats
¼ cup (60 mL) of quinoa, rinsed
¼ cup (60 mL) of amaranth
¼ cup (60 mL) of millet
2 tablespoons (30 mL) of chia seeds
2 tablespoons (30 mL) of freshly ground flaxseeds
1 teaspoon (5 mL) of cinnamon or nutmeg
¼ teaspoon (1 mL) of salt

For the pears
½ cup (125 mL) of white wine
2 tablespoons (30 mL) of honey
½ teaspoon (2 mL) of ground cardamom
2 Bosc or other firm pears, unpeeled, cored and diced

Start by making the porridge. Pour the water and honey into a medium pot and bring to a simmer over medium-high heat. Stir in the oats, quinoa, amaranth, millet, chia seeds, flaxseeds, cinnamon and salt. Return to a simmer and cook, stirring occasionally, until the grains are chewy and tender, 30 minutes or so.

Meanwhile, make the pears. In a small pot, bring the wine, honey and cardamom to a simmer over medium heat and cook until the mixture is reduced by half. Stir in the pears and continue to simmer until the pears are soft but not mushy and the syrup thickens noticeably, 3 or 4 minutes.

Scoop the porridge into serving bowls and top with a generous scoop of the pears.

Coconut Waffles with Lime Mango Yogurt

Waffles are in heavy rotation at our house, so I get to tinker with my recipe frequently. A tropical twist introduces the big flavour and rich nutrition of coconut to this breakfast classic. It's one of our favourites, especially when I make the yogurt the night before and freeze it. The promise of ice cream for breakfast can really get your sleepy gang going in the morning! If you're expecting a crowd, you can hold the cooked waffles in a 200°F (100°C) oven while you finish cooking the rest.

MAKES 12 TO 16 WAFFLES, SERVING 6 TO 8

For the yogurt

A 21-ounce (600 g) bag of frozen mango chunks
(or the juicy flesh of 6 ripe mangoes)
1 cup (250 mL) of full-fat plain, unsweetened yogurt
The zest and juice of 1 lime

For the waffles

2 cups (500 mL) of unsweetened shredded coconut
1½ cups (375 mL) of whole wheat flour
1½ cups (375 mL) of all-purpose flour
1 tablespoon (15 mL) of baking powder
½ teaspoon (2 mL) of salt
3 eggs
2 cans (14 ounces/400 mL each) of coconut milk
1 tablespoon (15 mL) of pure vanilla extract

Begin with the yogurt. In a food processor, blend the mango, yogurt and lime zest and juice until smoothly combined. If you have the time, freeze a batch the night before for even more excitement.

Next, make the waffles. Preheat your waffle iron. In a large bowl, whisk together the coconut, whole wheat flour, all-purpose flour, baking powder and salt. In a separate bowl, with the same whisk, mix together the eggs, coconut milk and vanilla. Add the wet ingredients to the dry, switch to a wooden spoon and with just a few quick strokes stir until a smooth batter forms.

Lightly spray the waffle iron with cooking spray. Spoon enough oozing batter into the centre to cover the cooking surface, then close the lid to spread it evenly. Cook until the waffles are lightly browned, 3 to 5 minutes. Repeat with the remaining batter. Serve with scoops of lime mango yogurt and share the first ones with whoever managed to get out of bed the fastest!

Bacon Cheddar Quiche in a Whole Wheat Crust

A classic quiche makes a delicious meal any time of day. If you're hesitant about your pastry skills, don't be! This recipe features a hearty whole wheat crust stirred together right in the pan. Easy! It also includes lots of luxurious bacon and cheddar, so it's excellent served with a small side salad for dinner too. **SERVES 6 TO 8**

For the crust
1½ cups (375 mL) of whole wheat flour
½ cup (125 mL) of vegetable oil or melted butter
2 tablespoons (30 mL) of water or milk
¼ teaspoon (1 mL) of salt

For the filling
4 thick slices of bacon, chopped
2 onions, thinly sliced
4 eggs
1 cup (250 mL) of milk
1 cup (250 mL) of whipping cream
2 green onions, thinly sliced
4 ounces (115 g) of aged cheddar, shredded
¼ teaspoon (1 mL) of salt
Lots of freshly ground pepper

Position a shelf just below the centre of your oven and preheat the oven to 350°F (180°C). Turn on your convection fan if you have one.

Start with the crust. Measure the flour, oil, water and salt directly into a 9-inch (23 cm) pie plate. Stir the works together with your fingers until evenly combined. The mixture will be slightly crumbly but hold together if pressed between your fingers. Use your fingers to firmly and evenly press about half of the dough up the sides of the pan to the top of the rim. Evenly press the remaining dough into the bottom of the pan, taking care not to make the corner where the sides and bottom meet too thick. Set aside.

Next, make the filling. Toss the bacon into a heavy skillet over medium-high heat. Add a splash of water to help it cook evenly. Cook, stirring frequently, until the water has evaporated and the bacon is deliciously browned and evenly crisp, 10 minutes or so. Strain out the bacon, leaving the fat behind, and scatter the crispy bits over the prepared crust.

Pour off most, half or none of the bacon fat. Toss in the onions and fry over medium heat, stirring frequently, until they're caramelized, 20 minutes or so. If you're in a rush, feel free to carry on as soon as the onions are tender and cooked through, before they're fully browned, just 5 minutes or so. Scatter the onions evenly over the bacon.

Whisk together the eggs, milk, cream, green onions, half of the cheese, and salt and pepper. Pour over the bacon and onions. Evenly top the works with the remaining cheese. Bake until the top is golden brown and the filling is firm, about 45 minutes. Cool for 10 minutes or so before slicing.

Veggie Skillet

Kick-start your day with a big boost of vegetables in this delicious skillet dish. This super-simple recipe is an easy way to add lots of flavour to your morning routine and an excellent way to meet your daily requirement of healthy vegetables. **SERVES 6 TO 8**

For the egg mixture

6 eggs

4 ounces (115 g) of Monterey Jack, grated

The leaves and tender stems of 6 sprigs or so of fresh thyme, minced

¼ teaspoon (1 mL) of salt

Lots of freshly ground pepper

For the vegetables

1 tablespoon (15 mL) of vegetable oil

1 pound (450 g) of baby potatoes, quartered

2 cloves of garlic, minced

1 zucchini, diced

1 yellow bell pepper, diced

1 red bell pepper, diced

1 red onion, finely diced

¼ teaspoon (1 mL) of salt

Lots of freshly ground black pepper

4 large handfuls of baby spinach

Start with the egg mixture. In a medium bowl, whisk together the eggs, half of the cheese, the thyme, salt and pepper. Set aside.

Heat the oil in a large nonstick skillet over medium-high heat. Add the baby potatoes and fry, turning and tossing occasionally, until they're crispy and golden brown, about 10 minutes. Add the garlic, zucchini, bell peppers, red onion, salt and pepper. Continue to cook, stirring frequently, just until their colours brighten and textures soften, another 5 minutes or so.

Reduce the heat to medium. Stir in the spinach just until the leaves wilt. Pour in the egg mixture and stir briefly until the eggs begin to set, a mere 30 seconds or so. Evenly scatter the remaining cheese over the top. Cover the skillet and cook until the eggs are firm and the cheese has melted, 2 or 3 minutes.

Homemade Breakfast Sausage

You can avoid the mystery ingredients in commercial sausages by making your own. You'll score an added bonus too: big, juicy flavour! Freeze a batch or two of cooked patties for speedy on-the-go convenience. They can easily be microwaved straight out of your freezer. Feel free to try 100% pork or turkey burgers instead of a blend. Both versions taste great. **MAKES 16 PATTIES, SERVING 8**

1 pound (450 g) of ground pork
1 pound (450 g) of ground turkey
2 or 3 tablespoons (30 or 45 mL) of maple syrup
2 tablespoons (30 mL) of fennel seeds

2 teaspoons (10 mL) of salt
1 teaspoon (5 mL) of dried thyme
1 teaspoon (5 mL) of dried sage
½ teaspoon (2 mL) of red chili flakes

Position racks in the upper and lower thirds of your oven and preheat the oven to 350°F (180°C). Turn on your convection fan if you have one. Line 2 baking sheets with parchment paper or silicone baking mats.

Sausage is best when everything is blended but you don't overmix and toughen the works. In a large bowl, with your hands, gently mix all the ingredients together until the meats and seasonings are evenly distributed. Divide into 16 equal portions. Shape into patties and place on the prepared baking sheets. You can freeze them at this point, then store in resealable plastic bags, or carry on cooking.

Bake the sausage patties until they're lightly browned, 15 minutes or so, rotating the baking sheets top to bottom and front to back halfway through. Frozen patties will take 20 minutes or so.

Granola Cookies

There's more than one way to get your granola fix and more than one time of day to do it. Morning, noon or night, these cookies are packed with all the whole-grain goodness of granola and just enough spiced cookie dough to hold the works together. They're a treat you can feel good about anytime! **MAKES 24 TO 30 COOKIES**

2 eggs

1 very ripe banana, mashed

¾ cup (175 mL) of honey

½ cup (125 mL) of Cinnamon Applesauce (page 257)

½ cup (125 mL) of coconut or vegetable oil

1 teaspoon (5 mL) of pure vanilla extract

1½ cups (375 mL) of whole wheat flour

¼ cup (60 mL) of ground flaxseeds

1 tablespoon (15 mL) of cinnamon

⅛ teaspoon (0.5 mL) of salt

3 cups (750 mL) of large-flake rolled oats

1 cup (250 mL) of unsalted roasted almonds, coarsely chopped

½ cup (125 mL) of unsweetened shredded coconut

½ cup (125 mL) of raisins

Position racks in the upper and lower thirds of your oven and preheat the oven to 350°F (180°C). Turn on your convection fan if you have one. Line 2 cookie sheets with parchment paper or silicone baking mats.

In the bowl of a stand mixer fitted with the paddle, beat together the eggs, banana, honey, applesauce, coconut oil and vanilla until thoroughly combined. In a separate bowl, whisk together the flour, flaxseeds, cinnamon and salt. With the mixer on slow speed, gradually add the flour mixture and beat until smooth. Toss in the oats, almonds, coconut and raisins and mix until everything is evenly combined.

Roll generous spoonfuls of dough in your hands to make 1-inch (2.5 cm) balls and arrange them fairly close together on the prepared cookie sheets (they won't spread much in baking). Press to about ½ inch (1 cm) thickness. Bake until firm and golden, 15 minutes or so, rotating the pans top to bottom and front to back halfway through. Transfer to racks to cool.

Real Fruit Roll-Ups

Apples are loaded with pectin, a magical ingredient that helps set jams and jellies and gives great strength and flexibility to homemade fruit roll-ups. In this recipe the apples get a strong nutritional boost from chia seeds, which also help the roll-ups hold together. What a great way to add a homemade healthy treat to a lunchbox! **MAKES 20 SNACKS**

2 pounds (900 g) or so of apples, cored and cut into large chunks

A 21-ounce (600 g) bag of frozen raspberries

A 1-inch (2.5 cm) knob of ginger, thinly sliced or grated

½ cup (125 mL) of water

2 tablespoons (30 mL) of chia seeds

Position racks in the upper and lower thirds of your oven and preheat the oven to 200°F (100°C). Turn on your convection fan if you have one. Line 2 baking sheets with lightly oiled parchment paper or silicone baking mats.

Toss the apples, raspberries and ginger into a medium saucepan, add the water and bring to a slow, steady simmer over medium-high heat. Cover and continue simmering until the apples are very soft, 20 minutes or so. Remove from the heat, stir in the chia seeds, cover and rest until the seeds absorb the liquid and swell, 10 minutes or so.

Process the mixture through the large holes of a food mill or remove the ginger slices and purée the works in your food processor or blender. Divide evenly between the prepared baking sheets, spreading evenly and thinly.

Bake for 2 hours, then check for doneness every 30 minutes or so. The mixture will thin noticeably and the surface will dry and become slightly sticky. The moisture content in apples varies, so this may take up to 4 hours total. Remove from the oven and cool completely. Trim away any excess paper around the edges of the fruit leather. Roll each sheet of fruit and paper into a tight log, then with a pair of kitchen scissors cut into pieces 1 or 2 inches (2.5 or 5 cm) wide. Store in a resealable plastic bag.

Moroccan Hummus with Lots of Veggie Dippers

Hummus is one of the world's great snacks. It's richly flavoured, easily prepared, easily shared, and when you make it yourself, inherently pure and nutritious. Chickpeas are pulses, edible seeds of the legume family, so they're packed with powerful protein and lots of fibre. They're the foundation of this formerly exotic, now mainstream snack that's fun to experiment with—there really are endless variations! This version is inspired by the flavours of Morocco, where hummus remains a staple.

MAKES 3 CUPS, ENOUGH FOR 6 OR 8 SNACKERS

A 19-ounce (540 mL) can of chickpeas, drained and rinsed

½ cup (125 mL) of tahini or almond butter

¼ cup (60 mL) of extra-virgin olive oil, plus more for garnish

¼ cup (60 mL) of orange juice

¼ cup (60 mL) of marmalade

1 tablespoon (15 mL) of harissa paste

1 teaspoon (5 mL) of cumin seeds

1 teaspoon (5 mL) of cinnamon

30 or 40 fresh mint leaves (from 6 or 8 sprigs)

The zest and juice of 2 lemons

¼ teaspoon (1 mL) of salt

Your choice of veggie dippers

Radish wedges

Carrot sticks

Celery sticks

Red pepper slices

Cherry tomatoes

Jicama slices

Kohlrabi wedges

Cauliflower florets

Broccoli florets

Snap peas

Zucchini batons

Blend everything smooth in your food processor. Fill a festive bowl with the hummus, drizzle the top with more olive oil and share with lots of veggie dippers.

Zucchini Bites

These crispy little vegetable bites are a guilt-free snack packed with big flavour. Zucchini rounds covered in deliciously browned panko crumbs and rich Parmesan—summer squash has never had it so good! Thankfully, it's easy to throw together another batch too, since as soon as you try these you're going to want more. **SERVES 6 TO 8**

3 to 4 ounces (85 to 115 g) of finely grated Parmigiano-Reggiano

1 cup (250 mL) of panko bread crumbs

¼ cup (60 mL) of minced fresh oregano (or 1 tablespoon/15 mL dried)

¼ teaspoon (1 mL) of salt

Lots of freshly ground pepper

2 large zucchini, sliced ¼ inch (5 mm) thick

¼ cup (60 mL) of olive oil

Position racks in the upper and lower thirds of your oven and preheat the oven to 400°F (200°C). Turn on your convection fan if you have one. Line 2 baking sheets with parchment paper or silicone baking mats.

In a shallow dish, thoroughly combine the Parmesan, panko, oregano, salt and pepper. In a medium bowl, toss the zucchini slices in olive oil until they're evenly coated. Dredge the zucchini slices in the panko mixture, pressing each firmly to help the crust adhere. Arrange evenly on the prepared baking sheets.

Bake until the topping is brown and crisp and the zucchini is cooked through, 20 to 30 minutes, rotating the baking sheets top to bottom and front to back halfway through. Serve as soon as you can get your fingers on them.

10 Popcorns

Good old-fashioned popcorn is a worthy treat full of whole-grain goodness. A freshly made batch is easily tossed with a multitude of fun flavours. We love this ritual as we gear up for family movie night. It's not junk when you make it yourself! **MAKES ENOUGH FOR 4 TO 6 SNACKERS**

For the popcorn
Vegetable oil
1 cup (250 mL) of popcorn kernels

Start by making a big batch of popcorn. Set a large pot over medium-high heat. Pour in a puddle of vegetable oil, enough to thinly coat the bottom. Pour in the popcorn kernels. Shake the pot a bit to evenly coat the kernels with the oil.

When a few kernels pop and escape from the pot, put the lid on slightly askew to allow the steam to vent. Listen carefully. The tempo of the popping will increase from sporadic to constant. When it begins to slow, put the lid on tight and turn off the heat. When the crescendo has stopped, pour the popcorn into the largest bowl you can find, making sure to discard any un-popped kernels.

For Buffalo Wing Popcorn
1 cup (250 mL) of butter
½ cup (125 mL) of Frank's Original or your favourite hot sauce
2 tablespoons (30 mL) of celery salt

In a small saucepan over medium heat, melt the butter with the hot sauce and celery salt. Pour over the hot popcorn while it's still in the pot, constantly tossing and stirring the works until the flavours are evenly distributed. The residual heat of the pot will help evaporate some of the butter's moisture, preventing the popcorn from becoming soggy.

For Lemon Pepper Popcorn
3 lemons
½ cup (125 mL) of extra-virgin olive oil
1 tablespoon (15 mL) of freshly ground pepper
½ teaspoon (2 mL) of salt

Zest the lemons over the fresh popcorn. Drizzle in the oil and season with the pepper and salt. Toss and stir the works together until the flavours are evenly distributed.

For Parmesan Rosemary Popcorn
½ cup (125 mL) of extra-virgin olive oil
1 cup (250 mL) of finely grated Parmigiano-Reggiano
The leaves of 4 sprigs of fresh rosemary, very finely chopped
½ teaspoon (2 mL) of salt
Lots of freshly ground pepper

Drizzle the oil over the popcorn as you toss and stir the works together. Add the Parmesan, rosemary, salt and pepper and continue to toss and stir until the flavours are evenly distributed.

recipe continues...

For Sriracha Lime Popcorn

2 limes
2 tablespoons (30 mL) of Sriracha sauce
2 tablespoons (30 mL) of olive oil

Zest the limes over the fresh popcorn. Stir together the Sriracha and olive oil. Drizzle over the popcorn as you toss and stir the works together, evenly distributing the flavours.

Everything Bagel Popcorn

½ cup (125 mL) of butter
¼ cup (60 mL) of white sesame seeds
¼ cup (60 mL) of poppy seeds
2 teaspoons (10 mL) of onion powder
2 teaspoons (10 mL) of garlic powder
1 teaspoon (5 mL) of salt
Lots of freshly ground pepper

In a small saucepan over medium heat, melt the butter with the sesame seeds, poppy seeds, onion powder, garlic powder, salt and pepper. Bring to a sizzle, then drizzle over the popcorn as you toss and stir the works together, evenly distributing the flavours.

For Pumpkin Spice Popcorn

½ cup (125 mL) of butter
1 teaspoon (5 mL) of cinnamon
¼ teaspoon (1 mL) of nutmeg
¼ teaspoon (1 mL) of ground cloves
¼ teaspoon (1 mL) of ground ginger
2 tablespoons (30 mL) of sugar

In a small saucepan over medium heat, melt the butter with the cinnamon, nutmeg, cloves and ginger until lightly sizzling. Drizzle over the popcorn as you toss and stir the works together, evenly distributing the flavours. Sprinkle with sugar for a final flourish of sweetness.

For PB&J Popcorn

¼ cup (60 mL) of butter
½ cup (125 mL) of your favourite jelly or jam
½ cup (125 mL) of smooth peanut butter

In a small saucepan over medium heat, melt the butter and jelly or jam together. Stir in the peanut butter until smooth. Drizzle over the popcorn as you toss and stir the works together, evenly distributing the flavours. (A batch can seem a little soggy at first but it crisps nicely as it rests—if it lasts that long.)

For Maple Bacon Popcorn

8 thick slices of bacon, thinly sliced crosswise
½ cup (125 mL) of maple syrup
¼ teaspoon (1 mL) of salt
Lots of freshly ground pepper

Toss the bacon into a heavy skillet over medium-high heat. Add a splash of water to help it cook evenly. Cook, stirring frequently, until the water has evaporated and the bacon is deliciously browned and evenly crisp, 10 minutes or so.

Pour off none, some or most of the bacon fat. Add the maple syrup, salt and pepper and bring the works to a simmer. Bubble away as the syrup absorbs the flavour of the bacon and smoothly combines with the bacon fat, just a moment or two. Remove from the heat. Drizzle over the popcorn as you toss and stir the works together, evenly distributing the flavours.

For Garam Masala Popcorn

½ cup (125 mL) of butter
1 teaspoon (5 mL) of ground cumin
½ teaspoon (2 mL) of cinnamon
½ teaspoon (2 mL) of ground coriander
½ teaspoon (2 mL) of ground cardamom
¼ teaspoon (1 mL) of ground cloves
¼ teaspoon (1 mL) of nutmeg

In a small saucepan over medium heat, melt the butter with the cumin, cinnamon, coriander, cardamom, cloves and nutmeg until lightly sizzling. Drizzle over the popcorn as you toss and stir the works together, evenly distributing the flavours.

For BBQ Popcorn

½ cup (125 mL) of butter
1 teaspoon (5 mL) of chili powder
1 teaspoon (5 mL) of ground cumin
½ teaspoon (2 mL) of onion powder
½ teaspoon (2 mL) of garlic powder
½ teaspoon (2 mL) of salt
¼ teaspoon (1 mL) of cayenne pepper

In a small saucepan over medium heat, melt the butter with the chili powder, cumin, onion powder, garlic powder, salt and cayenne until lightly sizzling. Drizzle over the popcorn as you toss and stir the works together, evenly distributing the flavours.

Brown Rice Rolls with Avocado and Shrimp

It's easy to make your own California rolls. Give it a shot and you'll be surprised how fast you get the hang of it. With a little practice, you'll be a master. While you're at it you might as well roll in the whole-grain goodness of brown rice. **SERVES 6 TO 8**

For the rice

2 cups (500 mL) of short-grain brown rice

4 cups (1 L) of water

2 tablespoons (30 mL) of sugar

2 tablespoons (30 mL) of rice vinegar

1 teaspoon (5 mL) of salt

For the shrimp

1 pound (450 g) of shrimp, peeled and deveined

2 ripe avocados

2 green onions, thinly sliced

2 teaspoons (10 mL) or so of Sriracha or your favourite hot sauce

For the rolls

8 sheets of nori seaweed

1 cucumber

Soy sauce

Pickled ginger

Wasabi paste

Begin by making the rice. Combine the rice and water in a medium saucepan and bring to a furious boil over high heat, stirring frequently. Cover, reduce the heat and, without lifting the lid, slowly simmer until the rice is tender, about 40 minutes. Remove from the heat and rest, covered, for 5 minutes. Meanwhile, in a small bowl stir together the sugar, rice vinegar and salt until dissolved. Transfer the rice to a large bowl. Drizzle in the vinegar mixture while gently stirring the rice, evenly coating the works but not stirring long enough to get it mushy. Spread the rice on a baking sheet to cool quickly.

Next, make the shrimp. Bring a large pot of salted water to a boil over high heat. Stir in the shrimp. Cover the pot, remove from the heat and let stand for 10 minutes. Strain out the shrimp and drain well. Scoop the avocado flesh into a medium bowl and mash it coarsely. Chop the shrimp into small pieces and stir into the avocado along with the green onions and hot sauce.

Set up your sushi rolling station with a very sharp chef's knife, a finger bowl of water and a bamboo sushi mat. If you don't have a sushi mat, cut a square of parchment paper or double-folded plastic wrap about 1 inch (2.5 cm) larger than a nori sheet.

Cut the cucumber into thin wedges as long as the width of the nori sheets. Lay a sheet of nori, shiny side down and with a long side closest to you, on the sushi mat. Wet your fingertips and spread a little less than 1 cup (250 mL) of the rice in a thin, even layer over the sheet, leaving a 1/2-inch (1 cm) border at the far edge. Lay a wedge or two of cucumber along the edge of the rice closest to you, then evenly top with some of the shrimp mixture.

Gently lift the mat and carefully roll the fillings over onto the rice. Continue rolling, compacting everything tightly together, folding back the leading edge of the mat as you go. Use your finger to lightly moisten the exposed edge of the nori with water. Finish rolling as the moist seaweed adheres to itself. Set the roll aside, seam side down. Repeat with the remaining ingredients, forming 6 to 8 sushi rolls.

Using a wet knife, slice each roll into 6 or 8 pieces and arrange on a festive platter. Serve with soy sauce, ginger and wasabi.

Soups
and
Salads

Roast Chicken Vegetable Soup

Nothing is more satisfying than a pot full of old-school chicken soup. It's a delicious way to squeeze the most meals possible out of a single chicken. Simply roast the chicken, shred the meat and simmer the bones into broth. Efficient and tasty! Bonus: you have a myriad of options when it comes to the grain (brown rice, wild rice, barley, wheat berries, rye, farro, etc.), the root veg (sweet potato, potato, parsnip, turnip, etc.) and the green vegetable (broccoli, peas, edamame beans, green beans, kale, Brussels sprouts or spinach). **SERVES 4 TO 6**

For the roast chicken
A whole chicken (3 to 4 pounds/1.4 to 1.8 kg)
Salt and lots of freshly ground pepper

For the chicken broth
8 cups (2 L) or so of water
3 onions, coarsely chopped
1 head of garlic, cloves sliced
4 or 5 sprigs of fresh thyme
2 bay leaves

For the soup
2 onions, chopped
2 carrots, chopped
2 stalks of celery, chopped
½ cup (125 mL) of your favourite grain
2 to 3 cups (500 to 750 mL) of root vegetable cut into bite-size pieces
1 teaspoon (5 mL) of salt
Lots of freshly ground pepper
2 to 3 cups (500 to 750 mL) of green vegetable cut into bite-size pieces
1 tablespoon (15 mL) of chopped fresh thyme, sage, rosemary or oregano (or 1 teaspoon/5 mL dried)

Preheat your oven to 350°F (180°C). Turn on your convection fan if you have one.

Place the chicken breast side up in a roasting pan. Season the chicken inside and out with salt and pepper. Roast until the chicken is lightly browned and an instant-read thermometer inserted in the thickest part of the thighs and breast registers at least 165°F (75°C), about 1 hour.

Remove the pan from the oven. Leave the chicken in the pan and with two pairs of tongs, pull the meat from the bones, shredding it into bite-size pieces and leaving it in the pan. Toss the bones into a large pot. Pour a cup (250 mL) or so of the measured water into the roasting pan and stir to dislodge and dissolve the flavourful drippings and dried bits in the bottom of the pan. Refrigerate the works.

Make the broth. Break the chicken bones into smaller pieces to nestle them easily in the pot. Add the onions, garlic, thyme, bay leaves and the remaining water. Bring to a furious boil, then immediately reduce the heat to a slow, steady simmer. Cover the pot tightly and simmer for an hour or so. Remove from the heat and rest for another half-hour or so. Strain the broth through a fine-mesh sieve into a large bowl.

Now make the soup. Rinse out the pot and return the broth to it. Add the onions, carrots, celery and your choice of grain and root vegetable. Season with salt and pepper. Bring to a furious boil, then immediately reduce the heat to a slow, steady simmer. Cook until the grains and vegetables are tender, about 45 minutes. Stir in the reserved chicken meat and juices. Add your choice of green vegetable and herb. Bring back to a simmer and cook until hot, another 5 minutes or so.

Mexican Tortilla Chicken Soup

This classic soup will satisfy your craving for the spicy, rich flavours of Mexico. It's thickened with cornmeal that fills your bowl with big, bright flavours. This is the sort of full-meal-deal soup that will surely become a go-to family favourite. **SERVES 6 TO 8**

For the soup

A splash of vegetable oil

6 or 8 boneless, skinless chicken thighs, diced

1 ½ teaspoons (7 mL) of salt

4 cups (1 L) of real chicken broth or water

A 28-ounce (796 mL) can of crushed tomatoes

2 onions, coarsely chopped

1 head of garlic, cloves smashed

1 chipotle pepper in adobo sauce

1 jalapeño pepper, seeded and coarsely chopped

1 tablespoon (15 mL) of dried oregano

1 tablespoon (15 mL) of chili powder

1 tablespoon (15 mL) of ground cumin

¼ cup (60 mL) of fine yellow cornmeal

To finish

A bag of your favourite corn tortilla chips

2 ripe avocados, peeled and diced

½ cup (125 mL) of sour cream

1 lime, cut into 8 wedges

A handful or two of fresh cilantro leaves

Begin the soup by browning the chicken. Heat a large pot over medium-high heat and splash in enough vegetable oil to thinly coat the bottom. Season the chicken with ½ teaspoon (2 mL) of the salt and place it in the hot oil. Cook the chicken until browned all over and thoroughly crispy, 5 minutes or so. Pour in the chicken broth to stop the browning and dissolve the pan's flavours.

Meanwhile, make the soup base. In a food processor or blender or in a bowl with an immersion blender, purée the tomatoes, onions, garlic, chipotle, jalapeño, oregano, chili powder, cumin and the remaining 1 teaspoon (5 mL) salt. Add to the soup pot and bring the works to a slow, steady simmer.

Stir continuously with a whisk while slowly pouring the cornmeal into the simmering soup, making sure there are no lumps. Simmer until the cornmeal softens and thickens the soup and the sunny southwestern flavours emerge, 15 minutes or so.

To finish, lightly crush a handful of tortilla chips into each serving bowl. Ladle in the soup and top with avocado, sour cream, a lime wedge and some cilantro. Finish with some more of the chips for a crunchy topping.

Vietnamese Pho Noodle Soup

In recent years this classic Southeast Asian meal-in-a-bowl has exploded in popularity. I'm not surprised. It's quite simply one of the world's best ways to fill a soup bowl. Pho combines long-simmered meaty complexity with a bright, fresh vegetable finish. It's irresistible. It's also a bit of a project, but take the journey and you'll be rewarded with a vibrant meal and the satisfaction of having made it yourself. You'll have no trouble finding oxtails at your meat counter or specialty or ethnic butcher. **SERVES 6**

1 boneless sirloin steak (8 to 10 ounces/225 to 280 g)

For the soup base
2 pounds (900 g) of meaty oxtail sections
1 pound (450 g) of chicken wings
1 tablespoon (15 mL) of vegetable oil
½ teaspoon (2 mL) of salt
12 cups (2.8 L) of water

For the aromatics
4 onions, coarsely chopped
2 knobs (4 inches/10 cm each) of ginger, unpeeled, sliced
1 head of garlic, cloves smashed
1 tablespoon (15 mL) of vegetable oil
12 whole star anise
5 whole cloves
3 cinnamon sticks
2 tablespoons (30 mL) of black peppercorns
2 tablespoons (30 mL) of coriander seeds
2 tablespoons (30 mL) of fennel seeds
¼ cup (60 mL) of fish sauce
1 tablespoon (15 mL) of brown sugar

To finish the soup
1 pound (450 g) of bean sprouts, rinsed well
1 small white onion, thinly sliced
1 lime, cut into wedges
A handful or two of fresh mint leaves
A handful or two of tender fresh cilantro sprigs
Hoisin sauce
Sriracha sauce
A 14-ounce (400 g) package of rice stick noodles
4 green onions, thinly sliced

Freeze the steak first. Trim the fat and gristle from the meat. Place the steak in a resealable freezer bag and roll the meat into a tight cylinder. Squeeze the air out of the bag and seal it tightly, preserving the log shape. Freeze until solid. This will make it easier to cut it into very thin, even slices.

Next, make the soup base. Position a rack near the top of the oven and preheat your broiler. Place the oxtails and chicken wings in a large bowl. Splash in the oil and sprinkle in the salt. Toss the works together until evenly coated and seasoned, then arrange evenly in a roasting pan. Broil, turning once or twice, until thoroughly and evenly browned, about 15 minutes. Watch carefully, turning, repositioning and removing as needed. Transfer the meats as browned to your slow cooker or a large soup pot.

recipe continues...

Pour 1 to 2 cups (250 to 500 mL) of water into the roasting pan and rest until the savoury goodness left behind by the meat dissolves. Pour this over the meats, then add the remaining water. Set the slow cooker to low and cook for 6 or 8 hours (or simmer slowly, covered, in the soup pot for 3 hours).

Next, prepare the aromatics. Preheat your broiler again. Line a baking sheet with parchment paper or a silicone baking mat. Toss the onions, ginger and garlic with the vegetable oil. Spread in a single layer on the prepared baking sheet. Broil, stirring occasionally, until the aromatics are nicely browned. Set aside.

In a medium skillet set over medium heat, combine the star anise, cloves, cinnamon, peppercorns, coriander seeds and fennel seeds. Toast the spices, shaking and shimmying the pan from time to time, until they are fragrant and have darkened slightly, just a few minutes. Stir the browned aromatics and toasted spices into the soup base. Cover and continue simmering gently for another 2 hours or so in the soup pot or the rest of the day in your slow cooker. Strain the broth into a bowl, reserving the meat pieces, and refrigerate both for later or carry on. Discard the aromatics and spices.

When you're ready to eat, prepare the bean sprouts, onion, lime, mint and cilantro and set out on platters alongside the hoisin and Sriracha. Skim off the fat from the surface of the broth. Pour the broth into a clean soup pot, stir in the fish sauce and brown sugar, and bring to a simmer. Bring another large pot of salted water to a boil.

Remove the steak "log" from the plastic bag and with a very sharp knife, carefully slice it as thinly as possible. If you find it difficult, rest at room temperature until soft enough to handle, 5 to 10 minutes. Separate each slice to prevent them from sticking together in the soup. Remove the oxtail and chicken meat from their bones and set aside the meat.

Cook the noodles. Drop the rice sticks into the boiling water and cook until tender and chewy, but not mushy, just 3 or 4 minutes. Drain the noodles and divide among 6 large soup bowls.

Top each bowl with the cooked meat, raw beef and lots of green onions. Ladle 1 ½ cups (375 mL) or so of the simmering soup base into each bowl and watch the raw beef poach. Serve with chopsticks and Chinese-style soup spoons. Share with the traditional garnishes.

Apple Mussel Soup with Bacon, Leek and Thyme

Mussels are not just packed with fresh flavour and loaded with healthy seafood goodness; they're also super easy to cook. Just steam them open and they immediately release an incredibly rich, briny broth as the meat within firms tenderly. In this recipe the mussels join classically delicious ingredients to fill your bowl with a soon-to-be family favourite. **SERVES 4 TO 6**

4 thick slices of bacon, chopped

2 large leeks (white and light green parts only), halved, thinly sliced and rinsed well

2 or 3 of your favourite apples, unpeeled, cored and diced

1 teaspoon (5 mL) of salt

Lots of freshly ground pepper

1 cup (250 mL) of white wine

1 cup (250 mL) of sweet apple cider or apple juice

5 pounds (2.3 kg) or so of fresh Prince Edward Island mussels, rinsed and drained

The leaves and tender stems of 4 or 5 sprigs of fresh thyme, finely minced

Toss the bacon into a large soup pot over medium-high heat. Add a big splash of water to help it cook evenly. Cook, stirring frequently, until the water has evaporated and the bacon is deliciously browned and evenly crisp, 10 minutes or so. Add the leeks and apples. Season with salt and pepper. Cook, stirring, until the vegetables soften, 5 minutes or so. Pour in the white wine and apple cider. Bring to a furious boil, then reduce the heat to a slow, steady simmer.

Add the mussels, cover the pot tightly and cook until the shells steam wide open and release their juices and the meat within is firm, 10 minutes or so. Remove from the heat and rest, uncovered, until the shells are cool enough to handle. Discard any mussels that didn't open. Use the first shell as a tool to pick the firm meat from all the rest, returning the meat to the broth. Discard most of the shells, saving a few for garnishing if you like. Return the broth to a simmer, stir in the aromatic thyme and serve immediately.

Red Lentil Soup

Red lentils are excellent for thickening soup. This humble Canadian-grown legume is loaded with nutritious flavour, and since they're split and hulled they easily break down into a smooth purée as they simmer. Red lentils are one of the most iconic ingredients in Indian cooking, so they're often paired with the complementary flavours in this recipe. **SERVES 6 TO 8**

2 tablespoons (30 mL) of coconut oil
1 tablespoon (15 mL) of curry powder
1 tablespoon (15 mL) of turmeric
1 tablespoon (15 mL) of cumin seeds
1 tablespoon (15 mL) of fennel seeds
1 tablespoon (15 mL) of coriander seeds
¼ teaspoon (1 mL) of red chili flakes
2 onions, diced

4 cloves of garlic, minced
1½ cups (375 mL) of red lentils, rinsed
4 cups (1 L) of low-sodium vegetable stock or water
A 14-ounce (400 mL) can of coconut milk
A 5-ounce (142 g) container of baby spinach
The zest and juice of 1 lemon
½ teaspoon (2 mL) of salt

In a large pot over medium heat, melt the coconut oil. Add the curry powder, turmeric, cumin seeds, fennel seeds, coriander seeds and chili flakes. Stir as their flavours brighten and intensify, just a minute or two.

Add the onions and garlic and continue to stir and cook until the onions are soft and translucent. Stir in the lentils, vegetable stock and coconut milk. Bring to a furious boil, then reduce the heat to a slow, steady simmer. Cook until the lentils are tender, 15 minutes or so. Remove from the heat.

If you prefer a smoother soup, vigorously whisk the soup to break down the lentils. For an even smoother texture, purée the works in a blender or with an immersion blender. At the last second, stir in the spinach until it wilts. Season with the lemon zest, lemon juice and salt.

Provençale Vegetable Soup with Almond Basil Pesto

Anywhere in the world, when farmers bring fresh vegetables to cooks, simple dishes like this soup are the result. This one is iconic because its flavours are particularly memorable. Imagine insanely delicious, intensely fresh vegetable broth swirled with big, bright basil pesto. You can taste how healthy it is! **SERVES 6 TO 8**

For the pesto

At least 50 big fresh basil leaves, from a big bunch or two

1 cup (250 mL) of finely grated Parmigiano-Reggiano

1 cup (250 mL) of unsalted roasted almonds

¼ cup (60 mL) of extra-virgin olive oil

¼ cup (60 mL) of water

3 or 4 cloves of garlic

½ teaspoon (2 mL) of salt

Lots of freshly ground pepper

For the soup

2 tablespoons (30 mL) of extra-virgin olive oil

1 leek (white and light green part only), halved, thinly sliced and rinsed well

2 carrots, diced

2 stalks of celery, diced

4 or 5 cloves of garlic, minced

2 zucchini, diced

8 ounces (225 g) of green beans, trimmed to 1-inch (2.5 cm) lengths

1 pint (500 mL) of cherry tomatoes

2 cups (500 mL) of orecchiette or orzo

A 28-ounce (796 mL) can of diced tomatoes

A 19-ounce (540 mL) can of navy beans, drained and rinsed

4 cups (1 L) of low-sodium vegetable stock or water

The leaves and tender stems of 4 or 5 sprigs of fresh thyme, minced

2 bay leaves

2 teaspoons (10 mL) of salt

Lots of freshly ground pepper

Start with the pesto. Place the basil, Parmesan, almonds, olive oil, water, garlic, salt and pepper in your food processor. Purée into a smooth, bright paste, pausing once or twice to scrape down the sides with a rubber spatula. Transfer to a jar and keep in the refrigerator for up to a week or so.

To make the soup, heat the olive oil in a large pot over medium heat. Add the leeks, carrots, celery and garlic and cook, stirring frequently, until their colours brighten and they smell delicious, 5 minutes or so. Stir in the zucchini, green beans, cherry tomatoes, pasta, diced tomatoes, navy beans, vegetable stock, thyme, bay leaves, salt and pepper. Bring to a furious boil, then reduce the heat to a slow, steady simmer. Cook until the pasta is al dente, tender but slightly chewy, about 15 minutes. Serve the soup with several heaping spoonfuls of pesto in every bowl. Use it all up—it makes the soup sing!

Pure Broccoli Soup

I love this soup because it elevates humble broccoli to the heights of cuisine by showcasing intense flavour that is often lost or hidden. The secret to this soup's bright taste and nutritional value? Extra broccoli. Minimal distraction from other flavours and the power of a blender help too. A bowl of this goodness just might change a few opinions of this trusty vegetable. **SERVES 4**

¼ cup (60 mL) of butter

2 onions, chopped

4 cloves of garlic, thinly sliced

2 large heads of broccoli, cut into florets and the stems cut into chunks

2 cups (500 mL) of water

1 teaspoon (5 mL) of salt

Lots of freshly ground pepper

Melt the butter in a soup pot over medium heat. Add the onions and garlic and cook, stirring frequently, until softened and fragrant, 2 or 3 minutes. Add the broccoli, water, salt and pepper. Bring to a furious boil, then reduce the heat to a slow, steady simmer. Cover and cook until the broccoli is bright green and tender, about 10 minutes.

Working in batches, purée the soup in a blender until ultra-smooth. (You can also use an immersion blender or food processor, but the soup won't be as smooth.) Reheat the soup briefly before serving.

Coconut Curry Sweet Potato Soup

Sweet potatoes add beautiful flavour and silky smoothness to any soup. The nutrient-dense root softens and purées easily, giving body, colour and flavour to many recipes. Here it's joined by wonderfully rich and tasty coconut milk. They're the perfect match for the aromatic curried flavours around them. It all adds up to a healthy, hearty bowl of soup. **SERVES 6 TO 8**

2 large sweet potatoes (about 2 pounds/900 g), peeled and grated

2 onions, chopped

2 carrots, chopped

2 cans (14 ounces/400 mL each) of coconut milk

2 cups (500 mL) of water

2 cloves of garlic, sliced

A 1-inch (2.5 cm) knob of frozen ginger, finely grated

2 tablespoons (30 mL) of curry powder

2 teaspoons (10 mL) of salt

1 teaspoon (5 mL) of Sriracha or your favourite hot sauce

Pile everything into a large pot. Bring to a furious boil over medium-high heat, then reduce the heat to a slow, steady simmer. Cover and cook until the vegetables are tender and your kitchen smells amazing, 15 minutes or so. Remove from the heat and purée with an immersion blender (or, working in batches, in a regular blender or food processor).

Creamy Tomato Soup with Grilled Cheese Sandwiches

These classics were once always homemade, hearty and real until someone figured out a way to pack soup into a can full of sodium and not much else while someone else stopped making cheese and started manufacturing it. Not anymore, though. We're back to doing it ourselves, making soup and grilled cheese sandwiches from scratch and enjoying true flavour once again. **SERVES 6 TO 8**

For the soup

2 tablespoons (30 mL) of butter

2 onions, chopped

2 carrots, chopped

4 cloves of garlic, sliced

½ teaspoon (2 mL) of salt

A 5.5-ounce (156 mL) can of tomato paste

½ cup (125 mL) of white wine

2 cans (28 ounces/796 mL each) of diced tomatoes

2 cups (500 mL) of tomato juice, real chicken broth or water

½ teaspoon (2 mL) of Sriracha or your favourite hot sauce

1 cup (250 mL) of whipping cream

For each sandwich

2 slices of whole-grain bread

A spoonful of softened butter

A few thick slices of aged cheddar or your favourite cheese

A few pickle slices

Start with the soup. In a large pot, melt the butter over medium-high heat. Stir in the onions, carrots, garlic and salt. Sauté until the veggies have softened and the onions are translucent, about 5 minutes. Add the tomato paste and stir constantly as it deepens in colour and flavour and evenly coats the vegetables. Add the white wine and stir thoroughly, dissolving the tomato paste from the bottom and sides of the pot. Stir in the diced tomatoes, tomato juice and hot sauce. Bring to a furious boil, then reduce the heat to a slow, steady simmer. Cover and gently bubble away for 20 minutes or so.

Remove from the heat and purée the soup with an immersion blender (or, working in batches, in a regular blender or food processor). Add the cream and reheat the soup over low heat.

To make the sandwiches, preheat your sandwich press, griddle or a large, heavy skillet over medium heat. Layer the cheese and pickles between bread slices. Spread soft butter on both sides of each sandwich. Lightly toast the sandwiches until the cheese melts and the bread is golden brown and crispy, turning as needed, 5 minutes or so. Cut the sandwiches in half and serve alongside a big bowl of steaming creamy tomato soup.

Roasted Tomato Gazpacho with Avocado Salsa

A chilly gazpacho is a time-honoured way to show off the amazing flavour of vine-ripe tomatoes. At peak tomato season the soup is made with raw, flavourful vegetables, but out-of-season store-bought tomatoes are usually rather bland. Roasting them adds tremendous depth of flavour so they can step up and anchor this delicious dish. If you can, make the soup in advance so it has time to chill, but in a crunch feel free to serve it warm. **SERVES 6 TO 8**

For the gazpacho

3 pounds (1.4 kg) of ripe tomatoes, quartered
1 large onion, diced
6 cloves of garlic, thinly sliced
¼ cup (60 mL) of extra-virgin olive oil
¼ teaspoon (1 mL) of salt
The zest and juice of 1 lemon
The zest and juice of 1 orange
¼ teaspoon (1 mL) of Sriracha or your favourite hot sauce

For the avocado salsa

A handful of tender fresh cilantro sprigs
2 avocados, peeled and diced
1 pint (500 mL) of cherry tomatoes, halved
1 jalapeño pepper, seeded and finely minced
¼ red onion, minced
The zest and juice of 1 lime
½ teaspoon (2 mL) of salt
Your very best extra-virgin olive oil, for garnish

Preheat your oven to 400°F (200°C). Turn on your convection fan if you have one.

Make the soup. Pile the tomatoes, onions and garlic into a 13- x 9-inch (3.5 L) baking pan. Drizzle with the olive oil, sprinkle with the salt and toss to coat well. Spread into an even layer. Roast, turning once or twice, until the onions and tomatoes have lightly browned and shrunk, about 1 hour. Remove from the oven and cool for a few minutes.

Transfer the works to a blender or food processor. Add the citrus zest and juice along with the hot sauce and purée until very smooth. Transfer to a bowl, cover tightly and refrigerate until cold. After an overnight rest the flavours and aromas of the soup will fully emerge.

Make the salsa just before serving. Reserve a few cilantro sprigs for garnish and chop the remainder. Toss together the chopped cilantro, avocados, cherry tomatoes, jalapeño, onion, lime zest and juice, and salt.

To serve, pour the soup into bowls. Mound a small pile of the salsa in the centre of each bowl. Top with a sprig of cilantro and drizzle with some olive oil.

My Famous Caesar Salad

My wife, Chazz, loves Caesar salad and I love making her happy, so I make this recipe often. The dressing is rich and bright, the croutons simultaneously crunchy and chewy. There's a problem with this flawless salad, though: you'll develop a very low tolerance for mediocrity when you eat out. The dining public is inundated with sub-par Caesar salads drenched with bottled dressing and artificial flavours. You'll secretly wish for your own. Homemade is always better! **SERVES 4 TO 6**

For the croutons

1 whole-grain baguette, cut into large bite-size cubes

¼ cup (60 mL) of water

¼ cup (60 mL) of extra-virgin olive oil

For the dressing

6 thick slices of bacon, thinly sliced crosswise

¼ cup (60 mL) of extra-virgin olive oil

¼ cup (60 mL) of Dijon mustard

4 or 5 cloves of garlic, peeled

A 2-ounce (50 g) can or jar of anchovies (12 fillets or so), drained

The zest and juice of 2 large, juicy lemons

1 tablespoon (15 mL) of honey

A dash or two of Sriracha or your favourite hot sauce

For the salad

3 hearts of romaine lettuce, sliced into bite-size pieces

The leaves of 1 large bunch of fresh basil

2 ounces (55 g) or so of Parmigiano-Reggiano, shaved with a vegetable peeler

Begin with the croutons. Preheat your oven to 375°F (190°C). Turn on your convection fan if you have one.

Toss the bread cubes in a large bowl while you sprinkle them with water until it's evenly absorbed. Continue tossing with the oil until it too is absorbed. Spread out on a baking sheet and bake, stirring at least once halfway through, until the croutons are crisp and thoroughly golden brown, 20 to 30 minutes. Cool on the baking sheet while you prepare the rest of the salad.

To make the dressing, toss the bacon into a saucepan over medium-high heat. Add a big splash of water to help it cook evenly. Cook, stirring frequently, until the water has evaporated and the bacon is deliciously browned and evenly crisp, 10 minutes or so. Strain out the bacon bits and reserve for garnish. Reserve the tasty fat.

Measure the oil, mustard, garlic, anchovies, lemon zest and juice, honey and hot sauce into your blender or food processor. Add the reserved bacon fat. Purée until smooth.

Make the salad. In a large salad bowl, toss together the romaine, basil leaves and croutons. Pour over the dressing and toss the works until the salad is evenly dressed. Top with the bacon and shaved Parmesan.

Baby Spinach Salad with Mango, Cashews and Lime Ginger Dressing

The very best salad dressings are packed full of balanced flavours like this one. Sour lime, sweet honey, spicy ginger and savoury, salty fish sauce combine in a powerfully flavoured dressing that's addictively delicious. If you're new to the wonders of fish sauce, this is a good place to start. Don't be put off by its intensity. Its mysterious taste adds unmistakable richness to the dressing. **SERVES 4 TO 6**

For the dressing

The zest and juice of 2 limes

A 1-inch (2.5 cm) knob of frozen ginger, finely grated

¼ cup (60 mL) of extra-virgin olive oil

1 tablespoon (15 mL) of toasted sesame seeds

1 tablespoon (15 mL) of honey

1 tablespoon (15 mL) of Dijon mustard

1 teaspoon (5 mL) of fish sauce

1 teaspoon (5 mL) of Sriracha or your favourite hot sauce

For the salad

A 5-ounce (142 g) container of baby spinach

2 ripe mangoes, peeled and cubed

1 carrot, peeled, then further peeled into ribbons

1 small red onion, thinly sliced

1 cup (250 mL) of roasted cashews

Make the dressing. In a jar, combine the lemon zest and juice, ginger, olive oil, sesame seeds, honey, mustard, fish sauce and hot sauce. Seal tightly and shake vigorously until smoothly combined. Refrigerate for up to a week.

Make the salad. In a large, festive salad bowl, combine the spinach, mangoes, carrot, red onion and cashews. Pour over the dressing and toss gently until the leaves are lightly and evenly coated.

Baby Kale and Sprouted Lentil Salad

You'll love this salad, not only because it's delicious but also because it packs a double whammy of nutritional superstars: dark green kale and home-grown lentil sprouts. Ounce for ounce, sprouts are one of the most nutrient-rich foods around. Once you get started sprouting your own, you'll realize how easy it is to add this health-food staple to your repertoire. You just can't beat the micronutrients and sweet, earthy flavour they bring to the salad. **SERVES 4**

For the sprouted lentils
¼ cup (60 mL) of green or brown lentils

For the dressing
2 tablespoons (30 mL) of cider vinegar
2 tablespoons (30 mL) of extra-virgin olive oil
1 tablespoon (15 mL) of honey
1 tablespoon (15 mL) of Dijon mustard
⅛ teaspoon (0.5 mL) of salt
Lots of freshly ground pepper

For the salad
A 5-ounce (142 g) container of baby kale (or 1 bunch of kale, thinly sliced)
2 carrots, peeled, then further peeled into ribbons
½ cup (125 mL) of sliced almonds, toasted
½ cup (125 mL) of pumpkin seeds, toasted
½ cup (125 mL) of raisins

Start sprouting the lentils 5 days in advance. Cut a small piece of mesh screen, about 4 inches (10 cm) square. Pour the lentils into a 1-quart (1 L) mason jar. Cover the jar's mouth with the screen and tighten on the screw ring (don't use the lid part). This will make it super easy to rinse and drain your sprouts. Fill the jar with water, drain it through the mesh and fill it again. Soak the lentils for 4 hours or so, then drain well.

Start a twice-daily routine for your lentils. Each morning and evening, gently fill the jar with fresh water, rinse the lentils, then drain well through the screen. Try not to let the lentils sit in the water. Rest the jar on its side on the kitchen windowsill. The lentils are starting to grow already, even though you can't see it.

Shortly after the first day, they'll begin to sprout. In just 2 or 3 days more, the sprouts will be about ½ inch (1 cm) long, with small green leaves forming on the ends. They're ready to eat now. To save them for later, swap the screen for the jar's lid and refrigerate for up to a week.

Make the dressing. In a small jar, combine the vinegar, olive oil, honey, mustard, salt and pepper. Seal tightly and shake vigorously until smoothly combined.

Make the salad. In a large salad bowl, combine the fresh lentil sprouts, baby kale, carrots, almonds, pumpkin seeds and raisins. Pour over the dressing and toss gently until the leaves are lightly and evenly coated.

Watermelon, Feta and Arugula Salad with Spicy Lime Dressing

Salads are at their best when they surprise and delight with well-balanced flavours and textures, which is why sweet watermelon, salty feta and spicy arugula are perfect companions. Toss them together with an intense lime dressing and I'm sure you'll agree! **SERVES 6**

For the dressing
The zest and juice of 2 limes
2 tablespoons (30 mL) of extra-virgin olive oil
2 tablespoons (30 mL) of honey
1 to 2 teaspoons (5 to 10 mL) of Sriracha or your favourite hot sauce
1 teaspoon (5 mL) of Dijon mustard
¼ teaspoon (1 mL) of salt

For the salad
1 watermelon (4 to 5 pounds/1.8 to 2.3 kg), cut into roughly 1-inch (2.5 cm) cubes
A 5-ounce (142 g) container of baby arugula
1 red onion, thinly sliced
4 ounces (115 g) of feta, crumbled
1 cup (250 mL) of toasted pistachios, cashews, pine nuts or your favourite nut
2 handfuls of fresh cilantro leaves
A handful of fresh mint leaves

Make the dressing. Whisk together the lime zest and juice, olive oil, honey, hot sauce, mustard and salt until smoothly combined.

In a large, festive salad bowl, toss together the watermelon, arugula, red onion, feta, nuts, cilantro and mint. Pour over the dressing and gently toss the works until everything is evenly combined.

Celery Root Slaw

Celery root is one of my all-time favourite vegetables, especially served raw like this. Its mildly aromatic flesh has a sweet, snappy crunch that makes it the perfect foil for this simple slaw. If you've not tried this delicious root vegetable, this recipe is a good place to start. **SERVES 4 TO 6**

For the dressing

A large handful of parsley leaves and tender stems

The leaves and tender stems of 4 sprigs of fresh tarragon

2 green onions, coarsely chopped

2 cloves of garlic, coarsely chopped

The zest and juice of 1 lemon

¼ cup (60 mL) of your best extra-virgin olive oil

1 tablespoon (15 mL) of Dijon mustard

1 tablespoon (15 mL) of prepared horseradish

½ teaspoon (2 mL) of salt

¼ teaspoon (1 mL) of Sriracha or your favourite hot sauce

For the slaw

1 celery root

2 tablespoons (30 mL) of capers, rinsed

Make the dressing. In your blender or food processor, combine the parsley, tarragon, green onions, garlic, lemon zest and juice, olive oil, mustard, horseradish, salt and hot sauce. Purée until the greens are finely chopped and the mixture is smooth, just a minute or so.

Prepare the celery root. Slice off the root end to create a flat, stable surface for it to rest on. Trim away the skin using curved downward slices, following the shape of the celery root. Finally, trim away the gnarly top. Rinse the root well to get rid of any lingering soil. Grate through the large holes of a box grater or using the grating disc of your food processor.

In a medium bowl, combine the celery root, capers and dressing. Toss everything together until the celery root is evenly coated with dressing. You may serve immediately but you'll find that an overnight rest in your refrigerator really develops the flavours and textures.

Curried Chickpea Salad with Apples, Cucumber and Raisins

This delicious yet simple salad is inspired by the classic flavours of mulligatawny soup, the dish made famous by returned Englishmen missing the bright flavours of India. This is the sort of vegetable salad that's equally at home on the salad bar or served as a side with the main dish.

SERVES 4 TO 6

For the dressing

The zest and juice of 1 lemon

½ cup (125 mL) of mayonnaise

1 heaping tablespoon (18 mL) of curry powder

1 tablespoon (15 mL) of honey

½ teaspoon (2 mL) of salt

¼ teaspoon (1 mL) of Sriracha or your favourite hot sauce

For the salad

A 19-ounce (540 mL) can of chickpeas, drained and well rinsed

1 English cucumber, seeds removed, diced

1 Granny Smith apple, diced

1 cup (250 mL) of slivered almonds, toasted

1 cup (250 mL) of shaved coconut

½ cup (125 mL) of raisins

In a large bowl, whisk together the lemon zest and juice, mayonnaise, curry powder, honey, salt and hot sauce until smooth. Stir in the chickpeas, cucumber, apple, almonds, coconut and raisins. Mix well to coat evenly with dressing. Serve fresh or rest in your refrigerator overnight to allow the flavours to further develop.

Soba Noodle and Edamame Salad with Ginger Miso Dressing

My kids love slurpy noodles of all sizes, shapes, types and origins. When the noodles arrive in a balanced salad like this one, they're so busy slurping the big, bright Asian flavours that they never seem to notice all the vegetables. Nor do they notice Mom and Dad smiling, secretly proud of their healthy appetites! **SERVES 4 TO 6**

For the dressing
2 tablespoons (30 mL) of vegetable oil
2 tablespoons (30 mL) of rice vinegar
2 tablespoons (30 mL) of any miso paste
2 tablespoons (30 mL) of honey
1 teaspoon (5 mL) of toasted sesame oil
1 teaspoon (5 mL) of Sriracha or your favourite hot sauce
A 1-inch (2.5 cm) knob of frozen ginger, finely grated

For the salad
2 bundles (about 6 ounces/170 g) of dried soba noodles
2 cups (500 mL) of shelled edamame beans
8 ounces (225 g) of bean sprouts, rinsed well
1 carrot, grated
4 green onions, thinly sliced diagonally
1 tablespoon (15 mL) of toasted sesame seeds

Make the dressing. In a small bowl, whisk together the vegetable oil, vinegar, miso paste, honey, sesame oil, hot sauce and ginger.

Bring a large pot of salted water to a boil over medium-high heat. Add the soba noodles and cook until just barely tender, about 3 minutes. Add the edamame beans and simmer for just 1 minute longer, then drain. Rinse the noodles and edamame with cold water and drain well.

In a large bowl, combine the noodles, edamame, bean sprouts, carrot, green onions and sesame seeds. Pour over the dressing and gently toss the works until everything is evenly mixed. Serve with chopsticks!

Millet Tabbouleh with Slow-Roasted Tomatoes and Lemon Oregano Dressing

Tabbouleh is for sharing. Equal parts grain and parsley, it has become a classic because it delivers a big dose of flavour and a big punch of nutrients. Plus, it's fun to enjoy with your friends and family. This version adds to the mix the wonderful nuttiness of millet. It too is loaded with whole-grain goodness. You'll love dressing up the bowl and putting it out for all to enjoy. **SERVES 6 TO 8**

For the tomatoes

8 Roma tomatoes, cut in half lengthwise

4 cloves of garlic, thinly sliced

2 or 3 tablespoons (30 or 45 mL) of extra-virgin olive oil

¼ teaspoon (1 mL) of salt

Lots of freshly ground pepper

For the salad

2 ½ cups (625 mL) of water

1 cup (250 mL) of millet

¼ teaspoon (1 mL) of salt

The leaves and tender stems of a big bunch of flat-leaf parsley, a few sprigs reserved for garnish, the remainder finely chopped

For the dressing

The zest and juice of 2 lemons

¼ cup (60 mL) of extra-virgin olive oil

2 tablespoons (30 mL) of honey

1 tablespoon (15 mL) of dried oregano

½ teaspoon (2 mL) of salt

Lots of freshly ground pepper

Roast the tomatoes. Preheat your oven to 300°F (150°C). Turn on your convection fan if you have one. Line a baking sheet with parchment paper or a silicone baking mat.

Arrange the tomatoes cut side up on the baking sheet. Evenly top them with the garlic slices. Drizzle with olive oil and season with salt and pepper. Bake until the tomatoes soften and shrink considerably and they look insanely delicious, 2 hours or so. Rest for a few minutes as the tomatoes cool and absorb their flavourful juices.

Meanwhile, make the millet. Bring the water to a boil in a small pot over medium-high heat. Stir in the millet and salt, cover tightly and reduce the heat to low. Simmer until the millet is cooked through and tender, 20 minutes or so. Remove from the heat and rest, covered, for 5 minutes or more. Spread the grains evenly on a baking sheet so they can cool quickly.

Make the dressing. Whisk together the lemon zest and juice, olive oil, honey, oregano, salt and pepper.

Put together the tabbouleh. Transfer the millet to a large, festive bowl. Stir in the dressing, coating the grains evenly, then toss in the parsley. Spoon the salad into an even mound and ring with the tomatoes and parsley sprigs.

Spaghetti Squash and Quinoa Salad with Savoury Dressing

A great salad draws together a group of interesting flavours, textures and colours and magically elevates them into something greater than the sum of its parts. This is one of those salads, and the fish sauce in the dressing is the savoury glue that binds everything together. If you're not familiar with fish sauce, here's your chance. Don't judge it by its name or the intense aroma in the bottle. This dish shows off its ability to mysteriously enhance all the ingredients without asserting itself. You'll see! **SERVES 6 TO 8**

For the salad
1 spaghetti squash (about 3 pounds/1.4 kg)
2 carrots, grated
1 cup (250 mL) of coarsely chopped unsalted roasted peanuts

For the quinoa
2 cups (500 mL) of water
1 cup (250 mL) of quinoa, rinsed
½ teaspoon (2 mL) of salt

For the dressing
The zest and juice of 1 lime
¼ cup (60 mL) of orange juice
¼ cup (60 mL) of fish sauce
1 tablespoon (15 mL) of honey
½ teaspoon (2 mL) of Sriracha or your favourite hot sauce

Preheat your oven to 400°F (200°C). Turn on your convection fan if you have one. Line a baking sheet with parchment paper or a silicone baking mat.

Cut the spaghetti squash in half lengthwise. Scoop out and discard the seeds. Place both halves of the squash on the prepared baking sheet cut side down to trap steam and help cook the flesh. Bake until the flesh becomes translucent and easily separates into long strands, about 45 minutes. When it's cool enough to handle, use a fork to scrape the strands into a large bowl. For the longest strands, scrape end to end.

While the squash bakes, make the quinoa. Bring the water to a boil in a small pot over high heat. Stir in the quinoa and salt, cover and reduce the heat to a slow, steady simmer. Cook until the quinoa is tender, 15 minutes or so. Remove from the heat and rest, without uncovering, until the grain finishes absorbing the moisture, 10 minutes or so.

Make the dressing by simply whisking together the lime zest and juice, orange juice, fish sauce, honey and hot sauce.

Add the quinoa, carrots, peanuts and dressing to the spaghetti squash. Stir and toss gently until everything is evenly coated with the dressing. Serve immediately or refrigerate for a few hours, even overnight, to allow the flavours to further develop.

Warm Farro and Roasted Vegetables with Roasted Garlic Lemon Dressing

Farro is an ancient grain, a relative of modern-day wheat that was once a staple of the Mediterranean diet. Its pleasant nuttiness, chewy texture and nutritional value have brought it back to prominence. In this salad it anchors a range of familiar flavours that are equally delicious served fresh today or refrigerated for tomorrow. **SERVES 6 TO 8**

For the roasted vegetables
1 fennel bulb, cut into small bite-size pieces
1 zucchini, cut into small bite-size pieces
1 red bell pepper, cut into small bite-size pieces
1 red onion, cut into small bite-size pieces
1 pint (500 mL) of cherry tomatoes, halved
1 head of garlic, cloves peeled and halved
2 tablespoons (30 mL) of vegetable oil
½ teaspoon (2 mL) of salt
Lots of freshly ground pepper

For the farro and salad
2 ½ cups (375 mL) of water
¼ teaspoon (1 mL) of salt
1 cup (250 mL) of farro, barley or other whole grain
The leaves of 1 bunch of fresh basil
2 green onions, thinly sliced

For the dressing
2 heads of garlic
The zest and juice of 2 lemons
¼ cup (60 mL) of extra-virgin olive oil
2 tablespoons (30 mL) of honey
¼ teaspoon (1 mL) of salt
Lots of freshly ground pepper

Begin by roasting the vegetables. Position racks in the upper and lower thirds of your oven and preheat the oven to 375°F (190°C). Turn on your convection fan if you have one. Line 2 baking sheets with silicone baking mats or parchment paper.

In a large bowl, combine the fennel, zucchini, red pepper, red onion, cherry tomatoes, garlic, oil, salt and pepper. Toss to coat the vegetables evenly with the oil. Divide the mixture between the prepared baking sheets and spread the veggies into a single layer. Nestle the 2 whole heads of garlic for the dressing in the midst of the works. Roast until the vegetables are caramelized and tender, 45 minutes or so. You don't need to stir them.

Meanwhile, cook the farro. Bring the water and salt to a boil in a small pot over medium-high heat. Stir in the farro and bring back to a simmer. Cover the pot, reduce the heat to low and cook until tender, about 20 minutes. Remove from the heat and rest, covered, while the farro finishes absorbing moisture, 10 minutes or so.

Make the dressing. Using a serrated knife, slice the tops off the roasted garlic heads. Squeeze the cloves out of their papery shells into a small bowl. Mash them well with a fork, then stir in the lemon zest and juice, olive oil, honey, salt and pepper.

In a large salad bowl, toss together the roasted vegetables, farro and dressing. Serve sprinkled with the basil and green onions.

Real Meals

Rosemary Roast Chicken and Potatoes

This is my favourite way to roast a chicken: perched on a thick bed of seasoned potatoes. It's that simple! The spuds absorb the roasting juices. The serving method is genius too. You can skip meticulous carving and instead simply shred the works right in the pan, serving an easily shared dinner packed with classic flavours. **SERVES 4**

For the potatoes

4 baking potatoes, each cut into 8 chunks

2 onions, diced

2 heads of garlic, cloves peeled

1 tablespoon (15 mL) of dried rosemary (or the minced leaves of a few fresh sprigs)

2 tablespoons (30 mL) of extra-virgin olive oil

1 teaspoon (5 mL) of salt

Lots of freshly ground pepper

2 or 3 green onions, thinly sliced

A handful of chopped fresh parsley

For the chicken

A large roasting chicken (3 to 4 pounds/1.4 to 1.8 kg)

1 teaspoon (5 mL) of salt

Lots of freshly ground pepper

2 or 3 sprigs of fresh rosemary

Preheat your oven to 375°F (190°C). Turn on your convection fan if you have one.

In a large bowl, toss together the potatoes, onions, garlic, rosemary, olive oil, salt and pepper until everything is evenly mixed. Transfer the works to a roasting pan, spreading it in an even layer.

Dry the skin of the chicken well with paper towels. Evenly season the outside and inside with salt and pepper. Place the whole rosemary sprigs inside the chicken and position the chicken breast side up on top of the potatoes. Roast until the potatoes are tender, the chicken is golden brown and an instant-read thermometer registers 165°F (75°C) in the thickest portion of the thigh, 60 to 90 minutes.

Remove the pan from the oven and rest the chicken for a few minutes. Leave the chicken on its perch and with two pairs of tongs tug and tear its meat directly into the potatoes along with the savoury juices. Reserve the bones to make a broth or discard. Sprinkle on the green onions and parsley. Stir everything together and serve in the pan.

Slow Cooker Chicken Dijon

When I need a head start with dinner I often take a few minutes in the morning to stuff my slow cooker with tasty ingredients. I love walking away knowing that when I return I'll have a delicious dish ready to serve. These French flavours complement each other beautifully. Classic aromatic vegetables, Chardonnay, Dijon mustard and sharp tarragon all combine into an eagerly awaited dinner. **SERVES 4 TO 6**

A splash of oil

A spoonful of butter

6 to 8 bone-in, skin-on chicken thighs

1 teaspoon (5 mL) of salt

Lots of freshly ground pepper

1 cup (250 mL) of Chardonnay or whatever red or white wine you happen to be drinking

4 potatoes, unpeeled, cut into large chunks

2 onions, cut into large chunks

2 carrots, cut into large chunks

2 stalks of celery, cut into large chunks

8 ounces (225 g) of button mushrooms, halved

3 cups (750 mL) of real chicken broth or water

½ cup (125 mL) of whipping cream

¼ cup (60 mL) of Dijon mustard

2 bay leaves

The leaves and tender stems of 6 or 8 sprigs of fresh tarragon, minced

If you have the time, brown the chicken. Heat a heavy skillet or sauté pan over medium-high heat with a splash of oil and a spoonful of butter. Season the chicken with salt and pepper and add to the sizzling butter. Sear until thoroughly browned on one side, then turn and continue. Remove from the heat and pour in the wine, swirling the pan gently. Rest the pan a few minutes as its browned flavours dissolve into the wine. Transfer the works to your slow cooker. (Alternatively, simply season the chicken with salt and pepper and place it in your slow cooker.)

Pile in the potatoes, onions, carrots, celery and mushrooms. Whisk together the chicken broth, cream and mustard (and the wine if you didn't brown the chicken), then pour over the works. Nestle in the bay leaves. Cover and cook on low until the chicken and vegetables are tender, about 6 hours. Carefully remove the chicken to a plate. Tease out the bones and cartilage, then return the meat to the slow cooker. For a fresh aromatic boost, stir in the tarragon just before serving.

Grilled Ratatouille with Chicken and Basil

When I fire up my grill, I love being able to cook an entire meal all at once. This dish is packed with summer flavours and can be served as either a hot dish or a cold salad. It combines the classic flavours of Provençal ratatouille with the charred deliciousness of the grill, all accented with bright lemon and basil. It's a hot-weather classic in my house. **SERVES 4 TO 6**

For the chicken

2 boneless, skinless chicken breasts

A splash or two of vegetable oil

½ teaspoon (2 mL) of salt

Lots of freshly ground pepper

For the ratatouille

1 eggplant, halved lengthwise

6 Roma tomatoes, halved lengthwise

4 zucchini, halved lengthwise

2 red onions, halved

2 red bell peppers, halved and seeded

¼ cup (60 mL) or so of grapeseed or vegetable oil

½ teaspoon (2 mL) of salt

Lots of freshly ground pepper

1 head of garlic

The zest and juice of 1 lemon

The leaves of 1 big bunch of fresh basil

Preheat your grill to the highest setting. Lightly oil the grates.

Get everything ready for the grill. Lightly oil the chicken and season with salt and pepper. Brush or rub the vegetables with oil and season with salt and pepper. With a serrated knife, trim the top from the head of garlic, rub with a bit of oil and wrap tightly in foil.

Get grilling. Start with the eggplant and garlic, which take the longest. Place the eggplant cut side down on the grate and nestle the garlic toward one side. After 10 minutes or so add the chicken, tomatoes, zucchini, red onions and red peppers. Cook, turning and flipping everything except the tomatoes and garlic, until the vegetables are tender and lightly charred and an instant-read thermometer inserted in the chicken registers at least 165°F (75°C), about 15 minutes more.

As the various ingredients finish cooking, remove and coarsely chop them, then transfer to a large serving bowl. Scoop the flesh of the eggplant from the skin and add to the other vegetables. Unwrap the garlic and squeeze out the softened cloves into a small bowl. Stir in the lemon zest and juice and pour over the vegetables. At the last second, roughly tear in the basil leaves and toss the works to combine the ingredients and flavours.

Chili Roast Chicken Wings

Chicken wings are always a hit at our table. My kids love them, and I love how simple they are to get into the oven. You don't need a deep-fryer to make them crispy and delicious. They're easy to experiment with too. I've tried every flavour under the sun. This version is one of our all-time favourites. **SERVES 4 TO 6**

½ cup (125 mL) of cornstarch
A generous ¼ cup (60 mL or so) of chili powder
¼ cup (60 mL) of sugar

1 tablespoon (15 mL) of salt
1 tablespoon (15 mL) of freshly ground pepper
24 whole chicken wings

Position racks in the middle and lower third of your oven and preheat the oven to 350°F (180°C). Turn on your convection fan if you have one. Line 2 baking sheets with silicone baking mats or parchment paper.

In a large bowl, whisk together the cornstarch, chili powder, sugar, salt and pepper. Add the chicken wings and toss until the tasty coating is evenly distributed. Arrange the wings on the baking sheets. Roast, without turning, and rotating the pans top to bottom halfway, until the wings are beautifully browned and tender, about 60 minutes.

Real Chicken Fingers with Chipotle BBQ Sauce

There's no shame in a meal of homemade chicken fingers, especially when they meet the high standards of finicky eaters. It's not junk food if you make it yourself. Your kids will think you're a hero, and you'll have the satisfaction of knowing dinner is made with real, wholesome ingredients.
SERVES 4 OR SO

2 large boneless, skinless chicken breasts

½ cup (125 mL) of whole wheat flour

1 egg, lightly beaten

¼ teaspoon (1 mL) of Sriracha or your favourite hot sauce

1 cup (250 mL) of panko bread crumbs

1 heaping tablespoon (18 mL) of chili powder

½ teaspoon (2 mL) of salt

Lots of freshly ground pepper

Preheat your oven to 425°F (220°C). Turn on your convection fan if you have one. Line a baking sheet with a silicone baking mat or parchment paper.

To cut the chicken fingers, remove the tender, the small muscle on the backside of each breast that easily detaches from the larger muscle. Using it as a guide, slice each breast further into 4 or 5 even pieces.

Set up a breading station with 3 bowls or shallow dishes. Add the flour to the first bowl. Whisk the egg and hot sauce in the second bowl. Stir together the panko and chili powder in the third. Bread the chicken pieces one at a time. To minimize mess, use one hand to handle them while they're moist and the other hand when they're dry. First, with your wet hand, transfer a chicken piece to the seasoned flour. With your dry hand, dredge it in the flour, tossing and turning until evenly coated, and dust off the extra flour. Drop into the egg and, using your wet hand, turn it to coat, then let the excess egg drip off. Finally, use your dry hand again to gently roll the chicken in the panko until evenly and thickly coated. Transfer the chicken to the prepared baking sheet.

To help the crust crisp, lightly spray each chicken piece with cooking spray. Bake until the chicken is cooked through and the crust is light golden brown, 20 minutes or so. Serve with Chipotle BBQ Sauce, page 248.

Sri Lankan Chili Chicken

This is one of the world's great chicken dishes. It's packed with authentic, aromatic flavour and just the right amount of spice to keep you interested and make it memorable. There's lots of sauce, so steamed rice is the perfect way to soak it up. **SERVES 4 TO 6**

For the aromatic flavour base

2 onions, coarsely chopped

4 cloves of garlic, smashed

2 to 4 green chilies, seeded and chopped

A 1- to 2-inch (2.5 to 5 cm) knob of ginger, unpeeled, thinly sliced

2 tablespoons (30 mL) of butter

2 tablespoons (30 mL) of curry powder

2 tablespoons (30 mL) of chili powder

2 lemongrass stalks, bruised with the spine of your knife and cut into roughly 3-inch (8 cm) lengths

1 cinnamon stick (or ½ teaspoon/2 mL ground)

6 green cardamom pods, lightly crushed (or ½ teaspoon/2 mL ground)

For the chicken

8 chicken drumsticks and thighs (or a whole chicken cut into 10 pieces)

2 red bell peppers, chopped

A 28-ounce (796 mL) can of diced tomatoes

2 teaspoons (10 mL) of salt

For the rice

1 cup (250 mL) of basmati rice

2 cups (500 mL) of water

½ teaspoon (2 mL) of salt

To finish

A 14-ounce (400 mL) can of high-quality coconut milk

The zest and juice of 1 lemon

A handful or two of chopped fresh cilantro, plus 4 to 6 sprigs for garnish

Begin with the aromatic flavour base. In a food processor or blender, pulse the onions, garlic, chilies and ginger until finely chopped. Melt the butter in a large, heavy pot or Dutch oven over medium heat. Add the onion mixture along with the curry powder, chili powder, lemongrass, cinnamon and cardamom. Cook, stirring frequently as the flavours emerge and brighten, 5 minutes or so.

Fill the pot with the chicken, red peppers, tomatoes and salt. Bring to a furious boil, then cover, reduce the heat to low and simmer until the chicken is tender, 45 to 60 minutes.

Meanwhile, make the rice. Stir the rice, water and salt together in a small pot and bring to a slow, steady simmer. Cover tightly and cook until tender, about 20 minutes. Remove from the heat and rest for 5 minutes or so before removing the lid.

To finish the chicken, stir in the coconut milk, lemon zest and juice, and chopped cilantro. (There's no need to remove the lemongrass and cinnamon stick.) Ladle the chili over bowls of steaming basmati rice. Garnish with cilantro sprigs.

Roast Chicken and Kale Hand Pies

Why would you take the time to roast a chicken, make dough, broth and a stew, then roll out, stuff and bake these hand pies? Because they're deeply satisfying and delicious, right? Well, yes, but they're also a great make-ahead meal. A batch in the freezer sets you up for a month of speedy suppers. Everything can be done in one afternoon, or in parts over two or three days.

MAKES 16 INDIVIDUAL PIES

For the roast chicken

A whole chicken (3 to 4 pounds/1.4 to 1.8 kg)
1 teaspoon (5 mL) of salt
Lots of freshly ground pepper

For the chicken broth

4 to 5 cups (1 to 1.25 L) of water
1 onion, coarsely chopped
4 sprigs of fresh thyme
1 bay leaf

For the dough

6 cups (1.5 L) of whole wheat flour
2 teaspoons (10 mL) of salt
1 cup (250 mL) of butter, cut into 1-inch (2.5 cm) cubes and frozen
2 eggs
1 cup (250 mL) or so of water

For the stewed filling

¼ cup (60 mL) of butter, softened
1 onion, chopped
2 stalks of celery, chopped
2 carrots, chopped
1 large bunch of kale, centre ribs removed and diced, leaves cut or torn into bite-size pieces
½ teaspoon (2 mL) of salt
Lots of freshly ground pepper
¼ cup (60 mL) of all-purpose flour
3 cups (750 mL) of real chicken broth
1 cup (250 mL) of whipping cream

Preheat your oven to 350°F (180°C). Turn on your convection fan if you have one.

Roast the chicken. Place the chicken breast side up in a roasting pan. Season the chicken inside and out with salt and pepper. Roast until the chicken is lightly browned and an instant-read thermometer inserted in the thickest part of the thighs and breast registers at least 165°F (75°C), about 1 hour.

Remove the pan from the oven. Leave the chicken in the pan and with two pairs of tongs, pull the meat from the bones, shredding it into bite-size pieces and leaving it in the pan. Toss the bones into a large saucepan. Pour a cup (250 mL) or so of the measured water into the roasting pan and stir to dislodge and dissolve the flavourful drippings and dried bits in the bottom of the pan. Refrigerate the works.

Make the broth. Break the chicken bones into smaller pieces to nestle them easily in the pot. Add the remaining water, onion, thyme and bay leaf. Bring to a furious boil, then reduce the heat to a slow, steady simmer. Cover the pot tightly and simmer for an hour or so. Remove from the heat and rest for another half-hour or so. Strain through a fine-mesh sieve into a large bowl, then discard the solids. Reserve the broth.

recipe continues...

Make the dough. In the bowl of a food processor, pulse together the flour and salt until combined. Add the butter and briefly pulse a few times until the mixture is mealy. Lightly whisk the eggs in a large measuring cup, then top up with enough water to measure 1½ cups (375 mL). With the motor running, slowly pour the egg mixture through the feed tube. Process just until the dough comes together. Tip the dough and any dried bits onto your work surface. Briefly knead the dough until it comes together into a smooth ball. Divide into 4 equal pieces, pat each into a flat rectangle and wrap tightly with plastic wrap. Refrigerate the dough for at least 30 minutes or overnight. (It can also be frozen in resealable freezer bags.)

Make the filling. Melt the butter in a large pot over medium-high heat. Add the onion, celery, carrots and kale stems and sauté until tender and aromatic, 5 minutes or so. Season with salt and pepper. Sprinkle the flour evenly over the vegetables and stir until evenly coated. Pour in the chicken broth and stir until it simmers and thickens. Stir in the cream, the reserved chicken meat and pan juices, and as much of the kale leaves as you can fit in the pot. Bring everything to a simmer and cook, covered and stirring occasionally, adding more kale leaves along the way, until all the kale is wilted and tender, 4 to 5 minutes. Remove from the heat and refrigerate until completely cooled, at least an hour or two or preferably overnight. (If you don't do this, the hot filling will melt the dough.)

Position racks in the middle and lower third of your oven and preheat the oven to 400°F (200°C). Turn on your convection fan if you have one. Line 2 baking sheets with silicone baking mats or parchment paper.

Lightly dust your work surface and the dough rectangles with flour. Let the dough soften for 5 minutes or so. Flour one rectangle of dough and the work surface a bit more along with a rolling pin. Roll the dough into a rectangle approximately 8 x 16 inches (20 x 40 cm). Every time you double the surface area of the dough, lightly dust it with flour and flip it over to prevent sticking. Cut into 4 rectangles, each 4 x 8 inches (10 x 20 cm). Spoon ¼ cup (60 mL) or so of the chilled filling onto one half of each rectangle, leaving a wide border of dough around the filling. (You may find it useful to keep the remaining filling in the refrigerator so it doesn't warm up as you work.) Fold the dough evenly over the filling. Align the edges, then pinch and roll along the seam to tightly seal it. With a sharp paring knife, cut 2 or 3 slits in the top of each pie to let the steam escape. Repeat with the remaining dough and filling. As you gain confidence try to stuff as much filling into each pie as you can. Arrange all 16 pies on the baking sheets.

Bake the pies, rotating the baking sheets top to bottom and front to back after 10 minutes, until they're thoroughly golden brown and steaming hot, another 10 minutes or so. Serve steaming hot from the oven. You can also cool a bit, then wrap and pack away for lunch later.

Chicken Stew Mashed Potato Casserole

One of life's great pleasures is a creamy chicken stew. My adaptation of this classic is a tasty casserole jazzed up by a delectable layer of mashed potatoes. There's just something about cutting through creamy potatoes and discovering a classic chicken vegetable stew beneath. This is comfort food at its best and an excellent dish to make ahead. The leftovers are good for days. **SERVES 10 TO 12**

For the chicken stew

4 thick slices of bacon, cut into ½-inch (1 cm) pieces

8 boneless, skinless chicken thighs (about 1 pound/450 g), cut into bite-size cubes

½ teaspoon (2 mL) of salt

Lots of freshly ground pepper

1 pint (500 mL) of button mushrooms, halved

2 onions, chopped

2 carrots, chopped

2 stalks of celery, chopped

4 cloves of garlic, minced

¼ cup (60 mL) of all-purpose flour

3 cups (750 mL) of real chicken broth or water

2 cups (500 mL) of frozen peas or green beans

1 cup (250 mL) of whipping cream

1 teaspoon (5 mL) of dried thyme

For the potato topping

6 large russet potatoes (4 pounds/1.8 kg or so), peeled and quartered

½ cup (125 mL) of milk

16 ounces (450 g) of aged cheddar, shredded

4 green onions, thinly sliced

Lots of freshly ground pepper

Preheat your oven to 400°F (200°C). Turn on your convection fan if you have one. Lightly oil a 13- x 9-inch (3.5 L) baking pan with cooking spray.

Toss the bacon into a large stew pot over medium-high heat. Add a big splash of water to help it cook evenly. Cook, stirring frequently, until the water has evaporated and the bacon is deliciously browned and evenly crisp, 10 minutes or so. Remove and reserve the bacon using a slotted spoon, leaving the flavourful fat behind. Season the chicken with salt and pepper. Working in batches if necessary to avoid crowding the pan, brown the chicken on all sides in the bacon fat, 5 minutes or so. Remove the chicken from the pot and set aside with the bacon.

Add the mushrooms to the pot. Cook, stirring them frequently until they release their moisture and brown a bit, 5 minutes or so. Add the onions, carrots, celery and garlic and sauté until tender and fragrant, another 2 to 3 minutes. Sprinkle the flour over the works and stir until absorbed. Slowly pour in the chicken broth, stirring constantly to prevent lumps. The mixture will be very thick at first but with constant stirring it will smooth out into a sauce. Add the bacon, chicken, peas, cream and thyme. Bring to a boil, then reduce the heat and simmer for 5 minutes or so. Pour the stew into the prepared baking pan.

Now make the potato crust. Bring a large pot of lightly salted water to a furious boil. Add the potatoes and reduce the heat to a slow, steady simmer. Cook until tender, about 15 minutes. Meanwhile, bring the milk to a simmer and remove from the heat. Drain the potatoes, return to the pot and mash thoroughly. Stir in the hot milk, cheese, green onions and pepper. Spread the works evenly over the chicken stew.

Place the casserole on a baking sheet to contain the inevitable drips. Bake until golden brown and bubbling, 20 to 30 minutes.

Roast Beef with Mushroom Gravy

Anyone can easily roast beef and make delicious gravy, especially if you keep in mind a few simple hints: (1) Searing meat doesn't seal in juices but it does create amazing flavours in the pan that eventually become deeply flavoured gravy. (2) The best way to roast meat to your desired doneness is to use an instant-read thermometer. (3) Let the meat rest before you slice it, thus giving the internal juices a chance to calm down so they don't flow out when you cut. (4) Try not to rest the meat on a flat surface or plate. The reduced surface tension actually encourages juice loss. Your best bet is a wire rack, but even propping the meat on a few chopsticks works well. (5) This recipe has delicious results with a sirloin tip, eye of round, outside round, inside round or rump roast. **SERVES 4 TO 6, WITH LEFTOVERS**

For the roast beef

A beef roast (2 to 3 pounds/900 g to 1.4 kg)
1 teaspoon (5 mL) of salt
Lots of freshly ground pepper
2 tablespoons (30 mL) of vegetable oil

For the gravy

2 tablespoons (30 mL) or so of butter
1 onion, chopped
2 cloves of garlic, minced
8 ounces (225 g) of mushrooms, thinly sliced
¼ cup (60 mL) of all-purpose flour
1½ cups (375 mL) of Beefy Broth (page 243) or water
½ cup (125 mL) of red wine
The leaves and tender stems of 2 sprigs of fresh thyme, minced

Preheat your oven to 325°F (160°C). Turn on your convection fan if you have one.

Cut the roast crosswise into two even pieces, thereby maximizing surface area, browning potential and delicious end cuts. Season thoroughly with salt and pepper. Heat the oil in a large, heavy skillet over medium-high heat. Brown the beef deeply and thoroughly on all sides, ignoring the smoke. This is your only shot at getting the rich, deep flavours that can only come from respectfully browned meat. Listen to the heat. A silent pan means nothing. A sizzle is the sound of flavour. Too loud, though, and a sizzling pan becomes a smoking-burning pan.

Transfer the skillet to the oven and roast until an instant-read thermometer registers 110°F (43°C) for rare, 120°F (50°C) for medium-rare to medium, 20 to 30 minutes. Transfer the beef to a wire rack set over a baking sheet to catch any drippings. Loosely cover with foil while you make the gravy.

Remembering that the handle may be hot, carefully measure the drippings in the pan. Add enough butter to bring the total to about ¼ cup (60 mL). Return the drippings and butter to the pan over medium-high heat and add the onions, garlic and mushrooms. Sauté as the vegetables soften, release their moisture and lightly brown, 5 minutes or so. Sprinkle in the flour and stir until it's fully absorbed. Pour in the broth and wine, stirring constantly until it heats through and thickens into gravy, about 5 minutes. At the last second, stir in the fresh thyme and any accumulated juices from the resting beef.

Root Vegetable Beef Stew

Every home cook needs a simple beef stew in their repertoire, a richly browned, deeply delicious broth of hearty beef, root vegetables, red wine and aromatic herbs. This tasty classic belongs up every cook's sleeve—complete with a few secrets: (1) The deeper the beef browning, the richer the stew's flavour. (2) You can use wine instead of long, laborious beef stock, like I've done in this recipe. (3) You can transform inexpensive tough cuts of beef into beautifully tender meat with a slow cooking time. (4) Finish with a last-second burst of fresh greens. (5) This recipe is especially versatile because you can use a mix of your favourite root veg: potatoes, sweet potatoes, carrots, parsnips, turnips, rutabaga, celery root, beets. **SERVES 6**

For the stew

2 or 3 tablespoons (30 or 45 mL) of vegetable oil

2 pounds (900 g) of stewing beef, cut into 1-inch (2.5 cm) cubes

1 teaspoon (5 mL) of salt

Lots of freshly ground pepper

2 to 3 pounds (900 g to 1.4 kg) of root vegetables, cut into bite-size chunks

2 large onions, cut into bite-size chunks

A 28-ounce (796 mL) can of diced tomatoes

1 bottle (750 mL) of big, bold red wine

2 or 3 bay leaves

1 head of garlic, cloves peeled and halved

1 tablespoon (15 mL) of dried rosemary (or the minced leaves of a few fresh sprigs)

1 teaspoon (5 mL) of salt

Lots of freshly ground pepper

To finish

2 tablespoons (30 mL) of prepared horseradish

2 cups (500 mL) of frozen peas

A 5-ounce (142 g) container of baby spinach, kale, chard or other savoury greens

Begin by browning the beef. Heat the oil in a large, heavy pot over medium-high heat until it's smoking hot. Toss the beef with salt and pepper. Working in batches to avoid crowding the pot, thoroughly and evenly brown the beef on all sides. Keep the works sizzling hot. Be patient and know that your reward will be deeper, richer flavour.

Return all the browned beef to the pot along with any accumulated juices. Add the root vegetables, onions, tomatoes, wine, bay leaves, garlic, rosemary, salt and pepper. Bring to a furious boil, then cover and reduce the heat to a slow, steady simmer. Cook until the beef and vegetables are meltingly tender, about 2 hours.

Finish by stirring in the horseradish, peas and greens. Turn off the heat, cover and rest as the greens wilt, just a minute or two.

Beefy Lentil Meatloaf

A good old-fashioned meatloaf is a great way to bring lots of beefy flavour to your table, especially when you slip in a few extra-healthy ingredients. Lentils add lots of fibre, protein and flavour, while chia and oats help keep the loaf moist and firm. Bottom line? Delicious, nutritious meatloaf.

SERVES 8 TO 12

For the meatloaf
½ cup (125 mL) of green lentils, rinsed
¼ cup (60 mL) of chia seeds
½ cup (125 mL) of water
2 pounds (900 g) of medium ground beef
2 eggs, lightly beaten
1 onion, finely chopped
4 cloves of garlic, minced
A 5.5-ounce (156 mL) can of tomato paste
1 cup (250 mL) of quick-cooking oats
¼ cup (60 mL) of dried oregano
2 tablespoons (30 mL) of ground cumin
1 teaspoon (5 mL) of salt
Lots of freshly ground pepper

For the sauce
¼ cup (60 mL) of brown sugar
¼ cup (60 mL) of ketchup
1 tablespoon (15 mL) of Dijon mustard
1 tablespoon (15 mL) of prepared horseradish

Preheat your oven to 375°F (190°C). Line a baking sheet with a silicone baking mat or parchment paper.

Begin by cooking the lentils. Bring a pot of water to a boil over high heat. Stir in the lentils and return to a simmer. Reduce the heat and simmer, uncovered, until the lentils are tender but not mushy, about 25 minutes. Drain well.

In a small bowl, stir the chia seeds into the ½ cup (125 mL) of water. Let sit for 10 minutes or so to allow the chia seeds to absorb the water and create a moisture-retaining gel.

Meanwhile, in a large bowl, combine the ground beef, eggs, onions, garlic, tomato paste, oats, oregano, cumin, salt and pepper. Add the lentils and chia gel. Mix the works well with your hands, evenly distributing the ingredients. Form into an evenly shaped loaf on the prepared baking sheet.

To make the sauce, in a small bowl, whisk together the brown sugar, ketchup, mustard and horseradish. Pour evenly over the meatloaf. Bake until the meatloaf is cooked through and browned, about 1 hour.

Moroccan Lamb Stew with Preserved Lemons and Pistachio Raisin Couscous

I've eaten lamb all over the world, but my favourite was in a Moroccan tagine. This stew is my homage to its mysterious aromatic flavours and wonderfully simple method. It's an easy way to transform an inexpensive lamb shoulder into a memorable meal and an authentic way to show off your homemade preserved lemons! (If you don't have preserved lemons, taste the stew at the end and stir in up to 1 teaspoon/5 mL of salt to compensate.) **SERVES 4 TO 6**

For the stew

2 pounds (900 g) of boneless lamb shoulder, cubed

2 onions, cut into bite-size chunks

4 carrots, cut into bite-size chunks

A 28-ounce (796 mL) can of crushed tomatoes

A 19-ounce (540 mL) can of chickpeas, rinsed and well drained

2 cups (500 mL) of real chicken broth or water

The zest and juice of 1 orange

4 cloves of garlic, minced

1 tablespoon (15 mL) of paprika

1 teaspoon (5 mL) of ground cumin

1 teaspoon (5 mL) of cinnamon

1 teaspoon (5 mL) of ground ginger

For the couscous

2 cups (500 mL) of water

1 teaspoon (5 mL) of salt

2 cups (500 mL) of couscous

1 cup (250 mL) of golden raisins or thinly sliced dried apricots

1 cup (250 mL) of unsalted dry-roasted pistachios

To finish and serve the stew

1 cup (250 mL) or so of your favourite green olives, pitted and quartered

2 to 3 tablespoons (30 to 45 mL) of Preserved Lemon Purée (page 253) (optional)

1 large bunch of fresh mint, 4 to 6 sprigs reserved, the remaining leaves finely chopped

Begin with the stew. In a large, heavy pot with a tight-fitting lid, combine the lamb, onions, carrots, tomatoes, chickpeas, chicken broth, orange zest and juice, garlic, paprika, cumin, cinnamon and ginger. Cover and bring to a furious boil, then immediately reduce the heat to a slow, steady simmer. Cook, without stirring, until the lamb and vegetables are tender, 90 minutes or so.

About 15 minutes before serving, make the couscous. In a medium pot, bring the water and salt to a boil over high heat. Stir in the couscous, raisins and pistachios. Cover, remove from the heat and rest until the couscous has absorbed the liquid and is tender, about 5 minutes.

To finish the stew, stir in the olives, preserved lemon purée and mint. Taste, and add more salt if needed. Pour a steaming ladleful or two of the stew over a mound of the couscous. Garnish with mint sprigs.

Pan-Fried Whitefish with Lemon Dill Tartar Sauce

This is my go-to method for quickly cooking up just about any fresh fish fillets. Simply dredge them in lightly seasoned flour and pan-fry in brown butter. Aromatic, herbaceous Old Bay Seasoning is perfect with fish. Look for it at your fishmonger's; if you can't find it, use chili powder, poultry seasoning, curry powder or your favourite spice blend. And nothing beats bright, lemony home-made tartar sauce alongside freshly pan-fried fish. **SERVES 4, WITH LEFTOVER SAUCE**

For the sauce
1 cup (250 mL) of mayonnaise
2 tablespoons (30 mL) of capers, rinsed
2 tablespoons (30 mL) of sweet green relish
2 tablespoons (30 mL) of chopped fresh dill
2 green onions, thinly sliced
The zest and juice of 1 lemon
Lots of freshly ground pepper

For the fish
1 cup (250 mL) of whole wheat flour
2 tablespoons (30 mL) of Old Bay Seasoning
½ teaspoon (2 mL) of salt
Lots of freshly ground pepper
2 tablespoons (30 mL) of vegetable oil
2 tablespoons (30 mL) of butter
4 whitefish fillets (6 ounces/170 g or so each)

Begin with the tartar sauce. In a bowl, whisk together the mayonnaise, capers, relish, dill, green onions, lemon zest and juice, and pepper. Cover and refrigerate until needed.

When it's time to cook the fish, in a shallow dish whisk together the flour, Old Bay Seasoning, salt and pepper. Place your favourite heavy skillet over medium-high heat. Pour in the oil, then toss the butter into the oil. The butter will melt and brown but the oil will help keep it from burning. Dip and dredge each piece of fish in the seasoned flour, evenly coating it on both sides. Knock off any excess and carefully slide into the hot fat. Cook, flipping once, until the fish is lightly browned and cooked through, about 2 to 3 minutes per side. Serve with heaping dollops of tartar sauce.

Mediterranean Baked Salmon with Tomatoes, Olives and Anchovies

This dish is filled with the big, bold, bright flavours of the sunny Mediterranean. With them you can gently cook fish and make a delicious sauce at the same time. You'll want to have a simple pot of steamed rice ready to soak up all the flavour of this beautiful meal! **SERVES 4**

For the fish

4 salmon fillets (4 to 6 ounces/115 to 170 g or so each) or 1 large fillet of salmon or whitefish

½ teaspoon (2 mL) of salt

Lots of freshly ground pepper

For the topping

1 pint (500 mL) of cherry tomatoes, halved

1 cup (250 mL) or so of Kalamata olives, pitted

1 red onion, diced

A 5.5-ounce (156 mL) can of tomato juice or a glass of red wine

A 2-ounce (55 g) jar or can of anchovies (8 fillets or so), drained and chopped

2 or 3 cloves of garlic, thinly sliced

1 tablespoon (15 mL) of capers, rinsed

1 tablespoon (15 mL) of dried thyme or oregano

1 tablespoon (15 mL) of olive oil

The zest and juice of 1 lemon

Lots of freshly ground pepper

Preheat your oven to 375°F (190°C). Turn on your convection fan if you have one.

Lightly season the fish with salt and pepper and nestle together in a 13- x 9-inch (3 L) baking dish, leaving a bit of space in between them. If using a large fillet, tuck under the thin tail to help it fit the pan. In a large bowl, thoroughly combine the cherry tomatoes, olives, red onions, tomato juice, anchovies, garlic, capers, thyme, olive oil, lemon zest, lemon juice and pepper. Spread the mixture over the fish. Cover the dish with foil, sealing the edges tightly. Bake until the fish is cooked through and tender, 30 minutes or so. Serve with steamed rice.

Fish Tacos with Cilantro Lime Chimichurri

I enjoyed my first fish taco off the beaten path in a Mexican beach town surrounded by locals. It was a revelation and I've been hooked ever since. Back home I prefer to make them without deep-frying the fish, and I think they're even tastier this way. These are a light, healthy way to anchor a fun meal, maybe even convert finicky fish eaters. It's amazing how much deliciousness and goodness you can cram into a simple tortilla! **MAKES 12 SMALL TACOS WITH SOME LEFTOVERS, SERVING 4 TO 6**

For the slaw
¼ cup (60 mL) of honey
¼ cup (60 mL) of white wine or cider vinegar
2 tablespoons (30 mL) of Dijon mustard
1 tablespoon (15 mL) of cumin seeds
½ teaspoon (2 mL) of salt
½ head of green cabbage, thinly sliced, shredded or grated
2 carrots, grated

For the chimichurri
½ bunch of flat-leaf parsley
½ bunch of fresh cilantro
2 or 3 cloves of garlic, peeled
1 jalapeño pepper, seeded

¼ cup (60 mL) of excellent olive oil
The zest and juice of 2 limes
¼ teaspoon (1 mL) of salt

For the tacos
1 cup (250 mL) of whole wheat flour
¼ cup (60 mL) of chili powder
½ teaspoon (2 mL) of salt
¼ teaspoon (1 mL) of cayenne pepper
2 tablespoons (30 mL) of grapeseed or vegetable oil
6 whitefish or salmon fillets (4 to 5 ounces/115 to 140 g each)
12 medium flour tortillas
12 to 24 tender fresh cilantro sprigs, for garnishing

Start with the slaw. In a large bowl or resealable container, whisk together the honey, vinegar, mustard, cumin seeds and salt. Add the cabbage and carrots and mix well. You can rest the works in the refrigerator for a day or two if you like.

Next, make the chimichurri. In a food processor or blender, blend the parsley, cilantro, garlic, jalapeño, olive oil, lime zest and juice, and salt until smooth. Reserve in a small jar for a day or two if needed.

When it's time to pan-fry the fish, preheat your oven to 200°F (100°C). In a shallow dish whisk together the flour, chili powder, salt and cayenne. Place your favourite heavy skillet over medium-high heat. Pour in the oil. Working in batches so you don't crowd the pan, dip and dredge each piece of fish in the seasoned flour, evenly coating it on both sides. Knock off any excess and carefully slide into the hot fat. Cook, flipping once, until the fish is lightly browned and cooked through, about 2 to 3 minutes per side. Keep the first batches warm in the oven while you cook the remaining fish.

Build the tacos. Cut each fish fillet in half crosswise. Lay a tortilla flat on a clean work surface. Place half a fish fillet in the middle, top with a big scoop of slaw and a generous spoonful or two of chimichurri. Garnish with a sprig or two of cilantro. Fold up and pass out straight away, or you can use an egg carton or two to help hold the folded tacos for a few minutes.

Paprika Pepper Shrimp and Rice

Paprika stars in this dish anchored by easily cooked shrimp. In no time at all you can cook a full meal of shrimp and vegetables that really shows off the sunny flavours of paprika. The spice is a mix of aromatic peppers, mildly spicy yet sweet. It can become stale and bland after too many months on the shelf, so you may need to crack a fresh bottle for this dish. **SERVES 4**

For the rice

1 cup (250 mL) of basmati, jasmine or other white rice

2 cups (500 mL) of water or real chicken broth

¼ teaspoon (1 mL) of salt

For the shrimp

1 red bell pepper

1 yellow bell pepper

1 orange bell pepper

2 tablespoons (30 mL) of vegetable oil

2 onions, thinly sliced

4 cloves of garlic, minced

2 to 3 jalapeño peppers, minced

2 tablespoons (30 mL) of paprika

1 teaspoon (5 mL) of salt

2 fresh tomatoes

1 pound (450 g) of shrimp, peeled and deveined

4 green onions, thinly sliced diagonally

The zest and juice of ½ lemon

Make the rice. Bring the water, rice and salt to a slow, steady simmer. Cover tightly, reduce the heat and simmer until the rice is tender, 15 minutes or so. Remove from the heat and rest, covered, 5 full minutes before removing the lid.

Meanwhile, cut each pepper in half from top to bottom. Scoop out the membranes and seeds. Tap each pepper half against your palm to knock out the last few seeds. Cut each half into as many top-to-bottom thin slices as you can.

Heat your largest skillet over medium-high heat. Splash in the vegetable oil. Add the onions, garlic, jalapeños, paprika and salt, stirring until the vegetables sizzle. Mix in the bell peppers and continue frying, stirring often, until the vegetables are cooked through and soft, 4 or 5 minutes. Grate the fresh tomatoes on the large holes of a box grater directly into the pan. Add the shrimp, clamp on the lid and continue cooking until they're cooked through and pink, 4 or 5 minutes more. Turn off the heat and stir in the green onions and lemon zest and juice. Serve over the rice.

Sausage Shrimp Jambalaya

This bayou classic is a reliable way to cram a meal with tons of flavour and please a crowd with the classic aromas of Louisiana. Jambalayas are great to have in your kitchen repertoire for when you want to liven things up with big flavours. You can anchor an entire party with a batch of this easy-to-make jambalaya or just jazz up an ordinary school night. Use the smaller amount of cayenne for pleasingly mild spice, or the larger amount for extra kick. **SERVES 6 TO 8**

2 tablespoons (30 mL) of vegetable oil

8 ounces (225 g) of andouille, chorizo or your favourite spicy sausage, sliced into thin rounds

4 stalks of celery, chopped

2 onions, chopped

1 green bell pepper, chopped

1 red bell pepper, chopped

4 cloves of garlic, minced

1 tablespoon (15 mL) of paprika

1 tablespoon (15 mL) of ground cumin

1 tablespoon (15 mL) of filé powder or dried thyme

¼ to ½ teaspoon (1 to 2 mL) of cayenne pepper

2 cups (500 mL) of medium-grain white rice

1 pound (450 g) of shrimp, peeled and deveined

A 28-ounce (796 mL) can of diced tomatoes

1½ cups (375 mL) of water

Heat a large, heavy pot or Dutch oven over medium-high heat. Splash in the vegetable oil, then toss in the sausage. Sauté until lightly browned, 2 or 3 minutes. Add the celery, onions, green and red peppers, garlic, paprika, cumin, filé powder and cayenne. Continue cooking until the vegetables are soft, 4 or 5 minutes.

Stir in the rice, coating the grains with oil and lightly toasting for a minute or so. Stir in the shrimp, tomatoes and water. Bring the works to a full boil, then reduce the heat to a simmer. Cover tightly and cook for 20 minutes or so. Turn off the heat and rest 10 full minutes without removing the lid. Uncover with a flourish.

Vietnamese Shrimp Banh Mi

In Vietnam, *banh mi* simply means "bread," a food introduced by the French during the country's colonial era. Today the term colloquially refers to sandwiches that have become an awesome example of fusion at its best. You don't have to go on vacation or even go out to enjoy one of the world's great sandwiches. Impress your friends and family in your own kitchen with a blend of flavours, textures and fun! **SERVES 4**

For the pickled carrots

2 carrots, coarsely grated

¼ cup (60 mL) of rice or cider vinegar

¼ cup (60 mL) of water

2 tablespoons (30 mL) of honey

For the Sriracha mayo

½ cup (125 mL) of mayonnaise

1 tablespoon (15 mL) of Sriracha or your favourite hot sauce

2 green onions, thinly sliced

For the shrimp filling

1 tablespoon (15 mL) of vegetable oil

1 small red onion, thinly sliced

2 cloves of garlic, minced

¼ teaspoon (1 mL) of red chili flakes

1 pound (450 g) of shrimp, peeled, deveined and coarsely chopped

1 tablespoon (15 mL) of fish sauce

1 tablespoon (15 mL) of honey

To build the sandwiches

A long, crispy baguette, cut into 4 pieces (or 4 crusty sub buns)

1 cucumber, halved crosswise and cut into long, thin slices

½ bunch of tender fresh cilantro sprigs

First, pickle the carrots. Place the carrots in a resealable container with the vinegar, water and honey. Cover tightly and shake until evenly mixed. Refrigerate for at least an hour, even overnight.

Make the Sriracha mayo by stirring together the mayonnaise, Sriracha and green onions in a small bowl. Cover and refrigerate for at least an hour, even overnight.

Cook the shrimp filling. Heat the vegetable oil in a skillet over medium-high heat. Add the onions, garlic and chili flakes. Sauté until the onions are soft and fragrant, 2 or 3 minutes. Add the shrimp and sauté until they are just cooked through, another minute or two. Remove from the heat and stir in the fish sauce and honey.

Make the sandwiches. Position a shelf near the top of your oven and preheat the broiler. Slice the baguette pieces along one side, cutting through until they open like a book. Toast, cut side up, until golden brown. Spread with Sriracha mayo and top with the shrimp, a few slices of cucumber, a scoop or two of drained carrots and a few sprigs of cilantro. Fold and devour.

Flaming Sambuca Pork Chops with Tomato Basil Pan Sauce

Drag a pair of pork chops through a simple seasoned flour, pan-fry them and stir up a quick sauce right in the pan. Classic, but not overly exciting. Try lighting the works on fire and add some *real* flavour! Welcome to the (simple!) art of flambéing. You'll love the way sambuca's anise-licorice notes complement the similar flavours in fresh basil. Everyone will love the show. **SERVES 4**

For the pork chops
¼ cup (60 mL) of whole wheat flour
1 tablespoon (15 mL) of dried thyme
1 tablespoon (15 mL) of garlic powder
1 tablespoon (15 mL) of onion powder
1 teaspoon (5 mL) of salt
Lots of freshly ground pepper
4 meaty pork chops, an inch (2.5 cm) or so thick, bone-in or boneless

1 tablespoon (15 mL) of vegetable oil
2 tablespoons (30 mL) of butter
1 ounce (30 mL) of sambuca or other anise-flavoured liqueur

For the pan sauce
½ cup (125 mL) or so of tomato juice
Lots of freshly ground pepper
A dozen or more fresh basil leaves

Begin with the pork chops. In a shallow bowl, whisk together the flour, thyme, garlic powder, onion powder, salt and pepper. Dip and dredge the pork chops in the seasoned flour until they're evenly coated.

Set your largest, heaviest skillet over medium-high heat and pour in the oil. Toss in the butter and swirl until melted and sizzling. Carefully add the pork chops and fry until thoroughly browned, 3 to 4 minutes on each side.

Ready for the show? Here's how to safely flambé the pork chops.

IF YOU'RE USING A GAS STOVE, swing the sizzling pan away from the flame, extend your arm and tilt the far edge of the pan down and away from you. Pour the sambuca into the tilted bottom, and with your arm still extended, slowly swing back halfway over the flame. Keep the pan tilted. Hold steady as the flame erupts in the pan.

IF YOU'RE USING AN ELECTRIC STOVE, pour the sambuca over the pork chops, shaking the pan to spread the alcohol around, and ignite by holding the edge of the pan near a lit candle.

When the flame and applause die down, add the tomato juice and pepper to the pan. Simmer, stirring, until the flavours mingle and the pork chops finish cooking, a few minutes longer. Remove the chops to a platter or plates and continue simmering until the sauce thickens. Meanwhile, stack the basil leaves, roll into a tight cylinder and thinly slice. When the sauce is ready, stir in the basil. Spoon the sauce over the chops.

Satay Pork Skewers with Sriracha Peanut Sauce

A simple skewer is an easy way to weave together meat and vegetables for a fun and enjoyable meal. Feel free to experiment with other firm fruits and vegetables. There are many, many flavours that you can mix and match in your kitchen this way! **SERVES 4**

For the marinade and dipping sauce

½ cup (125 mL) of real peanut butter, smooth or chunky

7 ounces (200 mL) of coconut milk

4 cloves of garlic, minced

The zest and juice of 2 limes

A 1-inch (2.5 cm) knob of frozen ginger, grated

1 tablespoon (15 mL) of honey

1 tablespoon (15 mL) of fish sauce

1 teaspoon (5 mL) of curry powder

1 teaspoon (5 mL) of Sriracha or your favourite hot sauce

¼ cup (60 mL) of chopped unsalted roasted peanuts

For the skewers

1 large pork tenderloin

2 red bell peppers, cut into 24 bite-size chunks

1 whole pineapple, trimmed and cut into 24 bite-size chunks

Soak 8 long wooden skewers in a bowl of water for an hour or so (or use metal skewers).

Make the marinade and dipping sauce. In a medium bowl, whisk together the peanut butter, coconut milk, garlic, lime zest and juice, ginger, honey, fish sauce, curry powder and Sriracha. To make the dipping sauce, transfer one quarter of the marinade to another bowl and stir in the chopped peanuts.

Skewer the pork. Trim away the white silverskin membrane on the fatter end of the tenderloin. Carefully slice the tenderloin lengthwise into 8 long, thin strips. On each skewer, thread a strip of meat around three pairs of pineapple and red pepper chunks, forming a serpentine of sorts. It's helpful to fold the thinner end over to strengthen it. (You may find it easier to trim each piece of pork crosswise into 3 chunks and simply alternate them on the skewer with the pineapple and peppers.) Arrange the completed skewers in a baking dish or pan and cover with the marinade, turning until evenly coated. Cover tightly and refrigerate for at least an hour, even overnight. If you don't have the time, you can carry on immediately.

Preheat your grill to medium-high. Lightly oil the grates with vegetable oil.

Grill the skewers, turning once or twice, until lightly charred and the pork is cooked through, about 10 minutes. Serve with the dipping sauce.

Spicy Ribs with Jalapeño Cheddar Cornbread

When your oven is stuffed with a couple of racks of meaty ribs slowly baking to deliciousness, you won't be able to stop thinking about them. To get your mind off the juicy flavour ahead, get a batch of zesty cornbread ready. The ribs will stay warm while you turn up the heat and bake away. These two are a match made in heaven! **SERVES 4 TO 6, WITH LOTS OF LEFTOVER CORNBREAD**

For the ribs
2 racks of baby back pork ribs
½ cup (125 mL) of brown sugar
½ cup (125 mL) of chili powder
1 tablespoon (15 mL) of ground cumin
1 tablespoon (15 mL) of ground oregano
1 tablespoon (15 mL) of onion powder
1 tablespoon (15 mL) of garlic powder
1 teaspoon (5 mL) of salt

For the cornbread
2 cups (500 mL) of yellow cornmeal
1 cup (250 mL) of all-purpose flour
¼ cup (60 mL) of sugar
1 tablespoon (15 mL) of baking powder
½ teaspoon (2 mL) of salt
1½ cups (375 mL) of milk
½ cup (125 mL) of butter, melted
2 eggs
6 ounces (170 g) of cheddar, shredded
4 to 6 jalapeño peppers, seeded and minced
4 green onions, thinly sliced
1 cup (250 mL) of frozen corn kernels, thawed
A couple handfuls of tortilla chips, crushed

Preheat your oven to 275°F (135°C). Turn on your convection fan if you have one.

Begin with the ribs. Most pork ribs have a tough, indigestible membrane—the fell—on the lean side. Use a spoon to loosen a corner of the membrane, then grasp it tightly and pull it all the way off. This will help the ribs cook evenly without curling. Fit them into a 13- x 9-inch (3.5 L) baking pan, overlapping as needed. To help them fit, cut each rack in half if necessary.

In a small bowl, whisk together the brown sugar, chili powder, cumin, oregano, onion powder, garlic powder and salt. Rub the spice mixture all over the ribs. Tightly cover the dish with foil. If your foil is not wide enough, place one long sheet of foil over another the same length. Fold over one long side by ½ inch (1 cm) and crimp tightly; fold and crimp another ½ inch (1 cm). Open up the two sheets into one larger one and tightly crease the centre seam. Cover the pan, crimping the edges tightly. Bake until the ribs are tender, about 4 hours. Take the ribs out of the oven and rest without removing the foil.

While the ribs bake, prep the cornbread. Spray another 13- x 9-inch (3.5 L) baking pan with cooking spray. In a large bowl, whisk together the cornmeal, flour, sugar, baking powder and salt. In another bowl, whisk together the milk, melted butter and eggs.

Once the ribs are out of the oven, increase the temperature to 400°F (200°C). Turn on your convection fan if you have one.

Finish mixing the cornbread. Pour the liquids into the dry ingredients and stir until no lumps remain. Fold in half of the cheddar, the jalapeños, green onions and corn. Pour into the prepared baking pan and smooth the top. Toss together the tortilla chips and the remaining cheddar and sprinkle over the batter. Bake until the top is brown and the cornbread is cooked through, 30 minutes or so. Serve with the ribs.

Slow Cooker Pulled Pork with Overnight Slaw

I never cease to be amazed at the transformative power of slow cooking. I love that with just a little patience, a tougher, inexpensive cut of meat can turn into a deeply satisfying meal. One of the best things about slow cooking is that it's just as easy to make a big batch, and then you're set with wonderful leftovers for the week! **MAKES 16 SANDWICHES**

For the slaw

¼ cup (60 mL) of honey

¼ cup (60 mL) of white or cider vinegar

2 tablespoons (30 mL) of Dijon or your favourite mustard

1 tablespoon (15 mL) of cumin seeds, lightly toasted

½ teaspoon (2 mL) of salt

½ head of green cabbage, thinly sliced

2 carrots, grated

For the pulled pork

2 onions, chopped

1 head of garlic, cloves minced

12 ounces (375 mL) of beer, tomato juice, orange juice, real broth or water

A 5.5-ounce (156 mL) can of tomato paste

¼ cup (60 mL) of honey

2 tablespoons (30 mL) of chili powder

1 tablespoon (15 mL) of ground cumin

1 tablespoon (15 mL) of ground oregano

1 teaspoon (5 mL) of cinnamon

1 teaspoon (5 mL) of salt

½ teaspoon (2 mL) of cayenne pepper

A bone-in pork shoulder (4 to 5 pounds/1.8 to 2.3 kg), skin removed

To finish

16 of your favourite crusty buns

Make the slaw. In a large bowl or resealable container, whisk together the honey, vinegar, mustard, cumin seeds and salt. Add the cabbage and carrots and mix thoroughly. Cover and refrigerate while the pork cooks or, for best results, overnight.

Slow-cook the pork. In your slow cooker, whisk together the onions, garlic, your liquid choice, tomato paste, honey, chili powder, cumin, oregano, cinnamon, salt and cayenne. Nestle the pork shoulder into the sauce, turning once or twice to evenly coat. Cover the slow cooker and set on low. After 6 or 8 hours, when the bone releases with no effort, remove the meat to a cutting board. Use two pairs of tongs to pull and shred the meat, mixing it back into the sauce.

Gather a crowd, pile on the pork and slaw and share the proceeds. Refrigerate any leftover slaw for up to a week. The pulled pork can be refrigerated for several days or frozen for a future meal.

Pork and Beans

This is rustic farmhouse cooking at its very best. Everyday ingredients, prepared simply, yet magically elevated into a deeply satisfying dish that has stood the test of time. The secret? The white beans become incredibly creamy and delicious when they slowly absorb the rich heartiness of an old-fashioned ham hock. **SERVES 6 TO 8**

3 cups (750 mL) of any dried white beans (about 1½ pounds/675 g)

2 onions, chopped

2 carrots, chopped

2 stalks of celery, chopped

1 head of garlic, cloves peeled and halved

1½ to 2 pounds (675 to 900 g) of smoked ham hocks

5 or 6 of your favourite fresh sausages

8 cups (2 L) of boiling water

2 bay leaves

Lots of freshly ground pepper

The leaves and tender stems of 6 sprigs of fresh thyme, finely minced

Soak the beans overnight in plenty of cold water. Choose a large container so they have lots of room to swell.

Preheat your oven to 350°F (180°C). Turn on your convection fan if you have one.

Drain the newly plump beans and rinse them well. Toss them into a large pot and stir in the onions, carrots, celery and garlic. Nestle the ham hocks into the middle of the works. Surround with the sausages. Pour in the boiling water and stir in the bay leaves and pepper. Cover tightly and bake until the ham bones release easily and the beans are tender and creamy, 4 hours or so. Carefully transfer the ham hock to a large plate or platter. Using a pair of tongs or a fork or two, pull away and discard the skin, bone and cartilage pieces. Return the meat to the pot and stir in the fresh thyme.

Whole Wheat Penne with Spinach and Tomato Bacon Sauce

This is my go-to pasta dish when I need a whole lot of flavour in a hurry. I can guarantee this meal will be devoured, and those pasta bowls emptied. As the pasta finishes up in the boiling water, feel free to toss in a few handfuls of green beans, peas, a chopped-up head of broccoli or any other favourite vegetable. **SERVES 4 TO 6**

8 slices of bacon, thinly sliced crosswise

2 onions, diced

4 or 5 cloves of garlic, minced

A 28-ounce (796 mL) can of crushed tomatoes

1 teaspoon (5 mL) of dried oregano, thyme or rosemary

½ teaspoon (2 mL) or so of Sriracha or your favourite hot sauce

1 pound (450 g) of whole wheat penne or your favourite pasta

A 5-ounce (142 g) container of baby spinach

Toss the bacon into a large saucepan over medium-high heat. Add a big splash of water to help it cook evenly. Cook, stirring frequently, until the water has evaporated and the bacon is deliciously browned and evenly crisp, 10 minutes or so.

Drain off none, some or most of the flavourful bacon fat. Add the onions and garlic and sauté with the bacon until they're soft, just 2 or 3 minutes. Stir in the crushed tomatoes, herb and hot sauce. Bring to a furious boil, then reduce the heat to a slow, steady simmer. Continue cooking until the flavours are fully developed, 10 minutes or so.

Meanwhile, bring a large pot of salted water to a furious boil. Add the pasta and cook until al dente, tender but slightly chewy, 10 minutes or so. Drain the pasta. Add the baby spinach to the pasta pot and top with the steaming pasta and the sauce. Stir together as the residual heat wilts the spinach, just a minute or two.

Pasta Alfredo with Lots of Green Veggies

This basic method uses one pot of boiling water to cook both the pasta and lots of green vegetables at the same time. Very convenient—and so is the sauce. But don't be fooled by the simplicity of true Alfredo sauce. It's one of the world's tastiest pasta sauces. **SERVES 4 TO 6**

For the sauce
¼ cup (60 mL) of butter
2 or 3 cloves of garlic, minced
1 cup (250 mL) of whipping cream
2 cups (500 mL) of grated Parmigiano-Reggiano (about 4 ounces/115 g)
½ teaspoon (2 mL) of salt
Lots of freshly ground pepper

For the pasta
1 pound (450 g) of your favourite pasta
1 bunch of broccoli, trimmed into bite-size florets
1 cup (250 mL) of fresh or frozen green beans, cut into bite-size lengths
1 cup (250 mL) of frozen edamame beans or green peas
A 5-ounce (142 g) container of baby spinach

Begin with the sauce. Melt the butter in a small pot over medium heat. Swirl gently as it melts, foams and lightly browns. Turn off the heat, add the garlic and stir until it's sizzling hot and fragrant, just 30 seconds or so. Pour in the cream. Stirring constantly, slowly add the Parmesan. Season with salt and pepper. Bring the sauce to a simmer over medium-low heat and stir until thickened, 3 or 4 minutes.

Meanwhile, bring a large pot of salted water to a furious boil. Add the pasta, and 5 minutes later add the broccoli and green beans. Continue cooking until the pasta is al dente, tender but slightly chewy, another 5 minutes or so. Stir in the edamame toward the end. Drain the pasta. Add the baby spinach to the pasta pot and top with the steaming pasta and the sauce. Stir together as the residual heat wilts the spinach, just a minute or two.

Cheddar Bacon Polenta with Lemony Arugula

This is my all-time favourite way to make polenta, which is really just a fancy name for cornmeal porridge. If you can make oatmeal, you can make polenta. The secret is to use lots of broth so that it's not too thick. While you're at it, you might as well stir in lots of flavours too. It's particularly delicious with a tangle of bright, snappy arugula on top. **SERVES 4 TO 6**

For the polenta

4 slices of bacon, thinly sliced crosswise

1 onion, chopped

4 cloves of garlic, minced

5 cups (1.25 L) of chicken broth, vegetable stock or water

¼ teaspoon (1 mL) of salt

Lots of freshly ground pepper

1 cup (250 mL) of cornmeal

1 tablespoon (15 mL) or so of minced fresh thyme leaves and tender stems

2 cups (500 mL) of shredded cheddar

For the arugula

A few handfuls of arugula

1 tablespoon (15 mL) of extra-virgin olive oil

The zest and juice of ½ lemon

Make the polenta. Toss the bacon into a medium pot over medium-high heat. Add a big splash of water to help it cook evenly. Cook, stirring frequently, until the water has evaporated and the bacon is deliciously browned and evenly crisp, 10 minutes or so.

Drain off all, some or none of the fat. Add the onions and garlic to the pot and sauté until they soften, 2 or 3 minutes. Pour in your liquid choice and add the salt and pepper. Bring to a furious boil, then reduce the heat to a slow, steady simmer. Whisking constantly to prevent lumps, slowly pour in the cornmeal. Switch to a wooden spoon and continue simmering, stirring frequently, until the cornmeal absorbs all the liquid and a thick, smooth polenta forms, 10 minutes or so. Stir in the thyme, then stir in the cheddar one handful at a time until the polenta is smooth. Divide evenly among serving plates.

Quickly and gently toss the arugula with the olive oil and lemon zest and juice. Top each plate of polenta with a small handful of arugula.

Tomato Mac 'n' Cheese

Few things in the kitchen are as delicious to eat or as simple to make as a bubbling pan of mac 'n' cheese. That's why I love trying different variations of the classic dish. In this version, tomatoes and oregano add lots of familiar flavour. Whatever version you make, though, nothing beats the satisfaction of doing it yourself! **SERVES 6 TO 8, WITH LOTS OF LEFTOVERS**

For the mac 'n' cheese

2 tablespoons (30 mL) of vegetable oil

2 onions, diced

4 cloves of garlic, minced

A 28-ounce (796 mL) can of crushed tomatoes

A 5.5-ounce (156 mL) can of tomato paste

1 cup (250 mL) of whipping cream

2 tablespoons (30 mL) of dried oregano

1 teaspoon (5 mL) of Sriracha or your favourite hot sauce

6 ounces (170 g) of Grana Padano or Parmesan, grated

1½ pounds (675 g) of whole wheat penne or your favourite pasta

1 pint (500 mL) of cherry tomatoes, halved

For the topping

6 ounces (170 g) or so of shredded mozzarella (about 2 cups/500 mL)

1 cup (250 mL) of panko or your favourite bread crumbs

Preheat your oven to 375°F (190°C). Turn on your convection fan if you have one. Lightly oil a 13- x 9-inch (3 L) casserole or baking dish with cooking spray.

First, make the sauce. Splash the oil into a large pot over medium-high heat. Add the onions and garlic and sauté until fragrant, 3 or 4 minutes. Stir in the crushed tomatoes, tomato paste, cream, oregano and hot sauce. Bring to a simmer, then reduce the heat. Whisk in the Grana Padano a handful at a time.

Meanwhile, bring a large pot of salted water to a furious boil. Toss in the penne, stir one or twice, and cook until the pasta is al dente, tender but slightly chewy, 10 minutes or so. Scoop out about ½ cup (125 mL) of the cooking water, then drain the pasta. Return the pasta to the pot along with the reserved cooking water, the sauce and the cherry tomatoes. Stir together well. Transfer to the prepared baking dish, spreading the works into a thick, even layer.

Stir together the mozzarella and panko and sprinkle evenly over the pasta. Bake until bubbling hot, golden brown and crisp, about 20 minutes.

Grilled Pizza with Sun-Dried Tomato Pesto and Mozzarella

You won't be surprised at how good these pizzas taste. I mean, grilled pizza just sounds amazing, doesn't it? You will also love how easy it is to grill a pizza. These are great to serve at parties, where your crowd will wolf these down. They're sure to end up on your top-ten list! **MAKES FOUR 10-INCH (25 CM) PIZZAS, WITH SOME LEFTOVER PESTO**

For the dough
3 cups (750 mL) of all-purpose flour
1 cup (250 mL) of whole wheat flour
1 package (2 ¼ teaspoons/11 mL) of instant yeast
1 teaspoon (5 mL) of salt
1 ½ cups (375 mL) of warm water
2 tablespoons (30 mL) of olive oil

For the pesto
1 cup (250 mL) of oil-packed sun-dried tomatoes, drained, reserving ½ cup (125 mL) of the oil
1 onion, coarsely chopped

¼ cup (60 mL) of unsalted roasted almonds
1 ounce (30 g) of grated Parmigiano-Reggiano
The leaves and tender stems of 1 bunch of fresh oregano
The leaves and tender stems of ½ bunch of parsley
¼ cup (60 mL) of tomato paste
Lots of freshly ground pepper

For the pizza
3 balls (½ pound/225 g each) of fresh mozzarella, thinly sliced
¼ cup (60 mL) of extra-virgin olive oil

Make the dough. Measure the all-purpose flour, whole wheat flour, yeast and salt into your food processor. Pulse once or twice to combine. With the motor running, slowly pour in the water and olive oil. Let the food processor run until the dough comes together into a ball that cleans the sides of the bowl. Turn the dough out onto a lightly floured work surface and lightly knead a few times. Transfer to a lightly oiled bowl, turning the dough to coat with oil. Cover tightly with plastic wrap and rest at room temperature until doubled in size, about 2 hours (or refrigerate overnight).

Make the pesto. Combine the sun-dried tomatoes, onions, almonds and Parmesan in a food processor. Pulse a few times until coarsely chopped. Add the reserved tomato oil, oregano, parsley, tomato paste and pepper, and process until smooth. Reserve.

Preheat your grill to the highest setting.

Divide the dough into 4 equal pieces. On a lightly floured surface, roll or stretch each piece of dough into a circle about 10 inches (25 cm) in diameter. Place each piece on individual pieces of parchment paper and stack on a baking sheet. Ready the rest of your pizza-making kit: 2 clean baking sheets, small bowl of olive oil, pastry brush, spoon, sliced mozzarella, tongs or BBQ spatula, maybe even a beer for the cook.

The size of your grill will determine how many pizzas you can make at once. Brush one pizza crust with olive oil and, with the help of the parchment paper, flip the dough oil side down onto the grate. Close the lid and grill until the bottom is crispy and lined with beautiful char marks, 3 minutes or so. Remove from the grill and rest briefly on a baking sheet. Brush the ungrilled top with oil. Flip the crust over and cover the grilled top with about ¼ cup (60 mL) of sun-dried tomato pesto. Evenly cover with mozzarella slices. Slide the pizza back onto the grill. Close the lid and grill until the bottom browns and the cheese melts, 5 minutes or so. Remove from the grill and repeat with the remaining pizza crusts.

Zucchini Chia Lasagna

This gluten-free pasta-less lasagna is layered with lots of thin zucchini "noodles" that easily support a load of vegetarian flavour. Zucchini can be quite watery, but no worries. Chia is a miracle super-food that not only absorbs the zucchini's moisture but adds a ton of nutrition too. **SERVES 6 TO 8**

For the tomato sauce

A 28-ounce (796 mL) can of crushed tomatoes

½ cup (125 mL) of chia seeds

2 tablespoons (30 mL) of olive oil

2 or 3 cloves of garlic, minced

The leaves of ½ bunch of fresh basil, chopped

½ teaspoon (2 mL) of salt

¼ teaspoon (1 mL) of red chili flakes

For the cheese sauce

2 eggs

½ cup (125 mL) of whipping cream

1 pound (450 g) of ricotta

4 cups (1 L) of shredded mozzarella

2 cups (500 mL) of grated Grana Padano or Parmigiano-Reggiano

Lots of freshly ground pepper

For the vegetable filling

2 tablespoons (30 mL) of vegetable oil

2 pounds (900 g) of white mushrooms, quartered

2 onions, chopped

4 cloves of garlic, minced

¼ teaspoon (1 mL) of salt

Lots of freshly ground pepper

A 5-ounce (142 g) container of baby spinach

For assembly

4 or 5 small or 2 or 3 large zucchini, cut lengthwise into long, thin strips

½ cup (125 mL) of chia seeds

2 cups (500 mL) of shredded mozzarella

The leaves of ½ bunch of fresh basil, for garnishing

Preheat your oven to 350°F (180°C). Turn on your convection fan if you have one. Spray a 13- x 9-inch (3 L) casserole or baking dish with cooking spray and place it on a baking sheet to contain any spills.

Make the tomato sauce. In a bowl, simply stir together the crushed tomatoes, chia seeds, olive oil, garlic, basil, salt and chili flakes.

Make the cheese sauce. In a medium bowl, whisk the eggs, then whisk in the cream and ricotta until smooth. Stir in the mozzarella and Grana Padano. Season with pepper.

Make the vegetable filling. Pour the oil into your largest, heaviest skillet over medium-high heat. Toss in the mushrooms, onions and garlic. Season with salt and pepper and sauté until the mushrooms release their moisture. Continue as that moisture cooks away and the vegetables lightly brown, 10 to 15 minutes in total. Stir in the spinach until it wilts. Remove from the heat.

recipe continues...

Begin Operation Lasagna Build. Assemble in the casserole dish in the following order:

- 1 cup (250 mL) of tomato sauce
- ⅓ of the zucchini slices
- ¼ cup (60 mL) of chia seeds
- ½ of the vegetable filling
- ½ of the cheese sauce
- ½ of the tomato sauce
- ⅓ of the zucchini slices
- ¼ cup (60 mL) of chia seeds
- Remaining vegetable filling
- Remaining cheese sauce
- Remaining zucchini slices
- Remaining tomato sauce
- All of the mozzarella

Fold a piece of foil big enough to cover the pan from corner to corner into a large triangle, unfold and fold again from the other two corners. Unfold, lightly spray with cooking spray, position over the lasagna sprayed side down, tenting the centre of the X over the works, and crimp the edges.

Bake the lasagna for 45 minutes, then remove the foil and continue baking until the cheese has browned beautifully and a knife easily pierces through the zucchini, another 15 minutes or so. Remove from the oven and rest as the chia finishes absorbing moisture and the lasagna cools and firms, 15 minutes or so. Just before serving, chop the fresh basil and sprinkle over the lasagna.

Meatless Monday Burrito Night

These burritos are so hearty and satisfying that no one will notice they don't have meat in their filling (unless you spill the beans!). They *will* notice all the bright, sunny southwestern flavours, though. In fact, why wait for Monday? They're perfectly delicious any day of the week! **MAKES 8 BURRITOS**

For the rice and bean filling
2 tablespoons (30 mL) of vegetable oil
1 onion, chopped
2 or 3 cloves of garlic, thinly sliced
1 tablespoon (15 mL) of chili powder
1 tablespoon (15 mL) of ground cumin
A 19-ounce (540 mL) can of red kidney beans or your favourite beans, drained and rinsed
A 28-ounce (796 mL) can of diced tomatoes
2 cups (500 mL) of water

1 cup (250 mL) of rice
1 chipotle pepper in adobo sauce, minced
1 teaspoon (5 mL) of salt

For the burritos
8 large whole wheat flour tortillas
2 cups (500 mL) of shredded cheddar
2 avocados, peeled and thinly sliced
A handful of fresh cilantro leaves

Make the rice and bean filling. Splash the oil into a medium pot over medium-high heat, then toss in the onions, garlic, chili powder and cumin. Sauté until the onions soften and the spices are fragrant, 3 or 4 minutes.

Stir in the kidney beans, tomatoes, water, rice, chipotle and salt. Bring to a furious boil, then immediately reduce the heat to a slow, steady simmer. Cover tightly and cook just long enough for the flavours to brighten and the rice to become tender, 15 minutes or so. Remove from the heat and rest, without uncovering, as the rice finishes absorbing the remaining moisture, 5 minutes or so.

Build the burrito. Position a big scoop of the rice and bean filling just below the middle of each tortilla. Top with cheddar, avocado and cilantro. Fold up the bottom, tuck in the sides and finish rolling the burrito as tightly as possible.

Sweet Potato Kale Stew with Peanut Sauce

What could be better than two nutritional powerhouses in the same dish? How about this dynamic duo with a smooth sauce? Sweet potato and kale anchor this recipe, but it's the deliciously balanced Asian peanut sauce that brings them together and elevates the dish to one that's addictively memorable! **SERVES 6 TO 8**

For the peanut sauce

½ cup (125 mL) of real peanut butter, smooth or chunky

7 ounces (200 mL) of coconut milk

The zest and juice of 2 limes

A 1-inch (2.5 cm) knob of frozen ginger, grated

1 tablespoon (15 mL) of honey

1 tablespoon (15 mL) of fish sauce

1 teaspoon (5 mL) of curry powder

1 teaspoon (5 mL) of Sriracha or your favourite hot sauce

¼ cup (60 mL) of chopped unsalted roasted peanuts

For the stew

2 large sweet potatoes (about 2 pounds/900 g), peeled and cut into bite-size pieces

1 large bunch of kale, centre ribs removed and thinly sliced, leaves cut or torn into bite-size pieces

2 cups (500 mL) of water

½ teaspoon (2 mL) of salt

Make the peanut sauce. In a medium bowl, whisk together the peanut butter, coconut milk, lime zest and juice, ginger, honey, fish sauce, curry powder, Sriracha and peanuts.

In a large soup pot, combine the sweet potatoes, sliced kale stems, water and salt. Bring to a furious boil over medium-high heat, then reduce the heat to a slow, steady simmer. Cover tightly and continue cooking, stirring occasionally, until the sweet potatoes are nearly tender, 10 minutes or so. Add the kale leaves, cover tightly and continue simmering until the leaves are bright green and tender, 3 or 4 minutes longer. Stir in the peanut sauce.

Vegetables, Grains and Sides

Sweet-and-Sour Red Cabbage

Red cabbage can absorb lots of flavours while retaining its wonderful texture. It's a hearty vegetable, so it pairs amazingly well with big, bold seasonings. You'll love its bright colour too; it's brought out by acidic vinegar reacting with purple pigments. **SERVES 4 TO 6**

1 head of red cabbage, halved, cored and thinly sliced

1 large red onion, thinly sliced

½ cup (125 mL) of cider or red wine vinegar

½ cup (125 mL) of water

4 to 6 tablespoons (60 to 90 mL) of honey or brown sugar

1 teaspoon (5 mL) of Sriracha or your favourite hot sauce

1 teaspoon (5 mL) of salt

½ teaspoon (2 mL) of cinnamon

¼ teaspoon (1 mL) of ground allspice

Pile everything into a large pot and bring to a furious boil. Reduce the heat to a simmer, cover tightly and cook, stirring occasionally, until the cabbage is tender, 30 minutes or so. Feel free to simmer another 15 minutes or more if you prefer a softer texture. Either way, at the last second, remove the cover, turn up the heat and stir until the last bit of moisture boils away, leaving glazed cabbage behind.

Grilled Asparagus with Chipotle Romesco Sauce

Of all the many ways of cooking asparagus, grilling is by far my favourite. Lightly charred asparagus adds a distinctive savoury flavour to any plate. Top with a spoonful of bright, tangy romesco sauce and you'll be hooked! **SERVES 4 TO 6**

For the romesco sauce

2 red bell peppers

1 cup (250 mL) of unsalted roasted almonds

1 cup (250 mL) of extra-virgin olive oil

¼ cup (60 mL) of red wine vinegar

2 tablespoons (30 mL) of tomato paste

A handful of parsley leaves and tender stems

2 cloves of garlic

1 chipotle pepper in adobo sauce

½ teaspoon (2 mL) of salt

For the asparagus

2 bunches of asparagus, woody ends trimmed

1 tablespoon (15 mL) of vegetable oil

½ teaspoon (2 mL) of salt

Lots of freshly ground pepper

Make the romesco sauce. Position a rack near the top of your oven and preheat the broiler. Line a baking sheet with foil.

Cut the red bell peppers in half and scoop out their seeds and membranes. Place cut side down on the prepared baking sheet. Broil the peppers until their flesh is tender and the skins are black and blistered, 5 minutes or so. Transfer them to a bowl and cover tightly with a plate. Rest until they're cool enough to handle, 10 minutes or so. Peel off and discard the skin.

Transfer the deliciously charred flesh and any accumulated juices to your food processor. Add the almonds, olive oil, vinegar, tomato paste, parsley, garlic, chipotle and salt. Process until smooth. Transfer to a bowl and set aside.

Preheat your grill on its highest setting. Toss the asparagus with oil, salt and pepper. Place the spears crosswise to the grates on your grill. Grill, turning occasionally with tongs, until they're tender and lightly charred, about 5 minutes. Arrange on a serving platter and spoon lots of romesco over top.

Beans and Sprouts with Sriracha Peanut Sauce

This easy recipe is a delicious way to transform a pile of vegetables into a special side dish. In the unlikely event you have leftovers, simply refrigerate the proceeds and you'll enjoy an equally tasty side salad tomorrow. **SERVES 6 TO 8**

For the sauce
1 cup (250 mL) of chopped unsalted roasted peanuts
½ cup (125 mL) of smooth real peanut butter
¼ cup (60 mL) of hot water
1 tablespoon (15 mL) of honey
1 tablespoon (15 mL) of fish sauce
1 teaspoon to 1 tablespoon (5 to 15 mL) of Sriracha sauce
The zest and juice of 1 lime

For the beans
1 pound (450 g) of green beans, trimmed and halved
2 cups (500 mL) of shelled edamame beans
1 pound (450 g) of bean sprouts, rinsed well

Make the sauce. In a small bowl, simply whisk together the peanuts, peanut butter, hot water, honey, fish sauce, Sriracha, and lime zest and juice.

Bring a large pot of lightly salted water to a boil over high heat. Add the green beans. A few minutes later add the edamame. Cook until the green beans are bright green and tender, about 5 minutes in total. Add the bean sprouts and stir until they're heated through, just a few moments. Drain well and return the vegetables to the pot. Pour in the peanut sauce. Stir everything together until the vegetables are evenly coated with the sauce.

Ginger Miso Steamed Bok Choy with Golden Tofu

This vegetarian side dish is hearty, delicious and nutritious enough to form an entire meal. It's anchored by the savoury richness that fermented soybeans bring to both the miso and tofu.

SERVES 4 TO 6

1 block (12 ounces/340 g) of firm or extra-firm tofu

2 tablespoons (30 mL) of vegetable or sesame oil

2 heaping spoonfuls (35 mL) of your favourite miso paste

¼ cup (60 mL) of water

2 cloves of garlic, smashed

A 1-inch (2.5 cm) knob of frozen ginger, grated

2 pounds (900 g) of regular bok choy, cut lengthwise into quarters, or baby bok choy, halved

Wrap the block of tofu in several layers of paper towel. Press firmly to absorb the surface moisture. Unwrap the block and cut in half lengthwise, then into ½-inch (1 cm) slices.

Heat the vegetable oil in a large pot over medium-high heat. Fry the tofu slices on one side, undisturbed, until you can see the golden brown creeping up the sides of the slices, 5 minutes or so. Flip the tofu and fry until the other side is golden brown, another 5 minutes or so.

Meanwhile, whisk the miso into the water to dissolve. When the tofu is done frying, add the miso water and lower the heat. Add the garlic and ginger. Simmer and stir for a moment or two to fully distribute the aromatic flavours. Add the bok choy. Cover tightly and steam until the bok choy is bright green, tender and aromatic, about 5 minutes.

Roasted Broccoli with Lemon Garlic Caper Butter

Bored with broccoli? Try roasting it! Roasted broccoli is a flavour revelation. Roasting infuses it with a delicious charred flavour that is further enhanced by the bright, garlicky flavour of the butter. When you're preparing this dish, you'll notice that larger heads of broccoli can have a tougher skin. If you don't enjoy the chewy texture, you can easily remove the fibrous skin. Make a small starter slit at the base end of the spears. Using the back of your knife, peel and tug the outer skin in long strips toward the crown. **SERVES 4 TO 6**

For the broccoli
2 heads of broccoli
2 tablespoons (30 mL) of vegetable oil
½ teaspoon (2 mL) of salt
Lots of freshly ground pepper

For the butter
¼ cup (60 mL) of butter
4 cloves of garlic, minced
The zest and juice of 1 lemon
1 tablespoon (15 mL) of capers, lightly chopped

Position an oven rack near the middle of your oven and preheat the broiler. Line a baking sheet with foil.

Cut each head of broccoli lengthwise into quarters, from the crown to the base. Arrange on the prepared baking sheet. Sprinkle with oil and with your fingers rub it around until all the surfaces are evenly coated. Sprinkle with salt and pepper. Roast, turning the broccoli once or twice to help it cook evenly, until tender and lightly charred, 15 minutes or so.

Meanwhile, make the butter. Toss the butter into a small pan over medium heat and swirl gently as it melts, foams and eventually forms a golden brown sediment. Make sure it doesn't burn! Turn off the heat and immediately stir in the garlic. (It will lower the temperature and prevent the butter from burning.) Stir in the lemon zest, juice and capers. To serve, spoon over the broccoli.

Pan-Roasted Brussels Sprouts with Chorizo

I grew up loathing Brussels sprouts. Then I became a chef, learned how to pan-roast and turned my life around. Today, roasted Brussels sprouts are one of my all-time favourite vegetables. (However, I still can't stand them boiled and mushy!) Pan-roasting is a classic restaurant trick. Busy line cooks speed things up by heating them on the stove before they go in the oven—searing heat before a finishing heat. A simple strategy for lots of golden brown flavour. **SERVES 4 TO 6**

2 pounds (900 g) of Brussels sprouts, trimmed and halved

8 ounces (225 g) of cured or fresh chorizo or your favourite spicy sausage, halved lengthwise and sliced

1 onion, thinly sliced

2 cloves of garlic, thinly sliced

2 tablespoons (30 mL) of vegetable oil

1 tablespoon (15 mL) of paprika

½ teaspoon (2 mL) of salt

Lots of freshly ground pepper

Preheat your oven to 400°F (200°C). Turn on your convection fan if you have one.

In a large bowl, toss together the Brussels sprouts, chorizo, onions, garlic, oil, paprika, salt and pepper. Heat your biggest, heaviest ovenproof skillet or sauté pan over medium-high heat. Add the vegetable mixture and cook, tossing frequently, until sizzling hot. Transfer the pan to the oven. Roast, stirring every 20 minutes or so, until the Brussels sprouts are lightly browned and tender, 45 to 60 minutes.

Spicy Basil Peperonata

This southern Italian dish is a delicious accompaniment to many summer meals and an excellent condiment for grilled meat or fish. The rich, aromatic sweetness that emerges from the slowly cooked bell peppers is beautifully balanced by the sour vinegar and spicy chili flakes. Enjoy fresh from the pan or refrigerate for a sandwich topping. **SERVES 6 TO 8**

4 onions, sliced

2 green bell peppers, cut lengthwise into eighths

2 yellow bell peppers, cut lengthwise into eighths

2 orange bell peppers, cut lengthwise into eighths

2 red bell peppers, cut lengthwise into eighths

8 cloves of garlic, thinly sliced

¼ cup (60 mL) of extra-virgin olive oil

1 teaspoon (5 mL) of salt

½ teaspoon (2 mL) of red chili flakes

2 teaspoons (10 mL) of red wine vinegar

The leaves of 1 bunch of fresh basil, thinly sliced

Preheat your oven to 375°F (190°C). Turn on your convection fan if you have one.

In a large bowl, toss together the onions, all the bell peppers, garlic, olive oil, salt and chili flakes. Pile the works into a 13- x 9-inch (3 L) baking or roasting pan. Bake, stirring every 30 minutes or so, until the peppers soften and their flavours concentrate, 90 minutes to 2 hours.

Stir in the red wine vinegar and fresh basil.

Grilled Corn with Spicy Lime Butter

You can grill corncobs in their husks to keep them juicy and sweet. The thick leaves protect the delicate kernels from the charring heat of the grill. You can also strip the cobs bare and enjoy the caramelized flavours of browned corn. Or get the best of both worlds by leaving a single layer of husk. You'll retain moisture and get the tasty brown too! **SERVES 4 TO 8**

½ cup (125 mL) of butter, softened

1 tablespoon (15 mL) of chili powder

1 tablespoon (15 mL) of Sriracha or your favourite hot sauce

The zest and juice of 1 lime

8 fresh cobs of corn in the husk

Preheat your grill to its highest setting. Lightly oil the grates.

Mix together the butter, chili powder, Sriracha and lime zest and juice until well combined.

Peel the corn as close to the cob as you can, leaving just the last innermost layer of the husk. Carefully peel back that husk without dislodging it, remove the silks, and replace the husk.

Grill the cobs, turning every few minutes, until the husk begins to pull away and the sweet kernels are tender and lightly charred. Pile on a platter for all to peel, and serve with the lime butter.

Greek Baked Eggplant

I love the way this decadent eggplant dish highlights so many of the iconic flavours of Greece's sunny cuisine. Slow baking allows the luscious texture of the eggplant to emerge. **SERVES 4**

2 large eggplants

¼ cup (60 mL) of extra-virgin olive oil

1 cup (250 mL) of crumbled feta

1 cup (250 mL) of Kalamata-style black olives, pitted and chopped

1 cup (250 mL) of oil-packed dried tomatoes, chopped

The leaves and tender stems of 1 bunch of fresh oregano, chopped

Lots of freshly ground pepper

Preheat your oven to 400°F (200°C). Turn on your convection fan if you have one.

Trim the stem tops from the eggplants and cut them in half lengthwise. Deeply score the flesh of each half in a 1-inch (2.5 cm) diamond pattern. Rub each cut side with 1 tablespoon (15 mL) of olive oil. Nestle them skin side down into a large baking pan.

In a bowl, stir together the feta, olives, tomatoes, oregano and pepper. Spread an even layer of the topping over the eggplants. Tightly cover the pan with foil and bake until the eggplant is meltingly tender and the crust has browned, about 90 minutes.

Carrots with Carrot-Top Pesto

Have you ever noticed how much delicious foliage a carrot produces as it grows in your garden? Carrot tops are a vegetable too, and here they're rightfully reunited with their below-the-ground partner. I've walked many years of garden rows and love the full-circle feel of this earthy dish.
SERVES 4 TO 6

For the carrots

2 bunches of carrots with their fresh tops attached

1 cup (250 mL) of water

½ teaspoon (2 mL) of salt

½ teaspoon (2 mL) of Sriracha or your favourite hot sauce

For the pesto

2 cups (500 mL) or so of tightly packed tender carrot tops, tough stalks trimmed away

½ cup (125 mL) of unsalted roasted almonds

¼ cup (60 mL) of olive oil

2 tablespoons (30 mL) of honey

The zest and juice of 2 lemons

2 or 3 cloves of garlic

½ teaspoon (2 mL) of Sriracha or your favourite hot sauce

¼ teaspoon (1 mL) of salt

Prep the carrots. Trim the tops from the carrots and reserve. Peel and trim the carrots. To cut them obliquely, cut across each carrot at a 45-degree angle. Rotate the carrot halfway and again cut through it at the same angle, creating wedge-shaped pieces with two angled cuts on one side. This gives the pieces a nice rustic look.

Toss the carrots into a pot and add the water, salt and hot sauce. Bring to a furious boil, then immediately reduce the heat to a slow, steady simmer. Cover tightly and cook until the carrots are tender, 5 to 10 minutes. Remove from the heat.

Meanwhile, make the pesto. Thoroughly wash the tender carrot tops. Drain well and press dry. Toss into your food processor. Add the almonds, olive oil, honey, lemon zest and juice, garlic, hot sauce and salt. Process, stopping the machine and scraping the sides once or twice, until finely puréed. Stir the pesto into the hot carrots. Serve hot or make ahead, refrigerate and serve as a salad.

Beets and Their Greens

Beets produce two equally delicious vegetables. Below the ground they're sweet and firm. Above the ground their greens are tender, mildly flavoured and incredibly nutritious. Together they're a marriage made in garden heaven. **SERVES 4 TO 6**

2 bunches of beets with their leaves attached
½ cup (125 mL) of water
2 tablespoons (30 mL) of honey
1 tablespoon (15 mL) of butter

1 tablespoon (15 mL) of red wine vinegar
½ teaspoon (2 mL) of Sriracha or your favourite hot sauce
¼ teaspoon (1 mL) of salt

Cut the beets into three separate piles: the greens, the stalks and the roots. Cut the greens into bite-size pieces. Cut the stalks into 1-inch (2.5 cm) lengths. Peel the roots and cut into bite-size halves, quarters or eighths, depending on their size. Rinse everything well but keep them separate.

Toss the beet roots into a medium pot and add the water, honey, butter, vinegar, hot sauce and salt. Bring to a boil over medium-high heat, then cover tightly and reduce the heat to a slow, steady simmer. When the beets are tender enough to easily pierce with a fork—after about 15 minutes—add the stalks. Continue simmering until the stalks are tender, another 10 minutes or so. Add the greens, cover, turn off the heat and rest until the greens have wilted, 2 or 3 minutes. Stir and serve.

Butternut Squash Apple Aloo Gobi

Aloo gobi means "potato cauliflower" in India, where it's a very common vegetable dish. It's so easy to make and such a hit at my table that I'm constantly creating variations of the original. This recipe replaces the firm potatoes with equally durable butternut squash. Apples add a delicious burst of sweetness, and you'll love the aromatic spice seeds. **SERVES 8 TO 10**

2 tablespoons (30 mL) of butter

2 cloves of garlic, minced

2 jalapeño peppers, seeded and finely diced

1 tablespoon (15 mL) of cumin seeds

1 tablespoon (15 mL) of fennel seeds

1 tablespoon (15 mL) of coriander seeds

2 tablespoons (30 mL) of curry powder

A 1-inch (2.5 cm) knob or so of frozen ginger, grated

1 teaspoon (5 mL) of salt

1 butternut squash, peeled, seeded and cut into bite-size pieces

1 head of cauliflower, cut into bite-size pieces

2 apples, cored and cut into bite-size pieces

½ bunch of fresh cilantro, chopped

Preheat your oven to 375°F (190°C). Turn on your convection fan if you have one.

Melt the butter in a small pan over medium heat. Add the garlic, jalapeños, cumin seeds, fennel seeds and coriander seeds. Stir for a minute or two, until the spices are lightly toasted. Remove from the heat and stir in the curry powder, ginger and salt.

In a large bowl, combine the butternut squash, cauliflower and apples. Add the spice mixture and toss together until everything is evenly combined. Transfer the works to a 13- x 9-inch (3 L) baking or roasting pan, spread it into an even layer and roast until the vegetables are tender and lightly browned, about 1 hour.

Just before serving, stir in and top with the chopped cilantro.

Garlic Mashed Potatoes

Ever order up garlic mash at a restaurant with the promise of big flavour only to be disappointed by the vaguest hint of garlic, leaving you craving more? Not when you're the cook in charge! These spuds are packed with enough garlicky goodness to satisfy your appetite for real flavour while establishing your credentials as the real deal in the kitchen. **SERVES 4 TO 6**

2 pounds (900 g) of your favourite potatoes, unpeeled, cut into large chunks

½ cup (125 mL) of butter

1 head of garlic, cloves minced

½ cup (125 mL) of milk

Bring a large pot of lightly salted water to a boil. Add the potatoes and cook until they're tender, about 20 minutes.

Meanwhile, make the butter. Toss the butter into a small pot over medium heat and swirl gently as it melts, foams and eventually forms a golden brown sediment. Make sure it doesn't burn! Turn off the heat and immediately stir in the garlic. (It will lower the temperature and prevent the butter from burning.) Stir in the milk and bring to a simmer.

Drain the potatoes thoroughly and return to the pot. Add the garlic mixture and mash until smooth.

Real French Fries

If you make your own french fries, they're not junk food, they're a treat, and you'll enjoy the satisfaction of doing them justice. Experts know that the crispest fries are cooked twice. First they're blanched at a relatively low temperature, then they're finished at a higher, crisping temperature. For truly decadent flavour, nothing tastes better than old-school lard! Make sure you use high-starch baking potatoes. **SERVES 4 TO 6**

6 large russet (baking) potatoes (about 4 pounds/1.8 kg), unpeeled

8 cups (2 L) of vegetable oil, grapeseed oil or lard

Salt

Pepper

Cut the potatoes into thick slices, then thin fries. Soak them in plenty of cold water for at least 30 minutes, even overnight.

Heat the oil in your largest, heaviest pot over medium heat. Fit the pot with a deep-fry thermometer. For maximum accuracy don't let it touch the bottom—it's best an inch or so up. Line 2 baking sheets with paper towels, one for the raw potatoes and the other for the cooked fries. Drain the soaked potatoes well, pat them dry and reserve on one of the prepared baking sheets.

Blanch the potatoes. Heat the oil to 300°F (150°C). Working in batches and stirring frequently, fry the potatoes until they soften and cook through, about 5 minutes or so. Your goal is to just barely cook the potatoes, saving the browning and crisping for the second fry. Use a slotted spoon to transfer them to the second baking sheet. Repeat with the remaining potatoes. At this time, the potatoes can be refrigerated or frozen.

When you're ready, crisp the potatoes. Line a baking sheet with paper towels. Heat the oil to 400°F (200°C). Working in batches, drop in the first batch of potatoes. The temperature of the oil will drop dramatically. Adjust the heat so it hovers around the sweet spot for golden brown flavour, 365°F (185°C). Stirring frequently, fry the potatoes until they're golden brown and crisp, 3 to 5 minutes.

Transfer the crisp fries to a large bowl and immediately sprinkle with salt and pepper, tossing to coat the works evenly. (Season while they're still hot so the salt and pepper will adhere well.) Share while you make the next batch. Reheat the oil to 400°F (200°C) before frying the next batch.

Vegetarian Lentil Poutine

Earthy lentils are hearty enough to anchor this flavourful gravy. Both the lentils and the mushrooms are wonderfully savoury. You'll be too busy enjoying this vegetarian poutine to miss the meat!

MAKES 8 CUPS (2 L) OF GRAVY, ENOUGH FOR 8 SERVINGS OF POUTINE

For the mushroom lentil gravy
¼ cup (60 mL) of vegetable oil
1 pound (450 g) of mushrooms, quartered
1 onion, chopped
4 cloves of garlic, minced
2 cups (500 mL) of red lentils
5 cups (1.25 L) of water
1 cup (250 mL) of red wine
4 sprigs of fresh thyme
1 bay leaf
1 teaspoon (5 mL) of salt
Lots of freshly ground pepper

For the poutine
1 batch of Real French Fries (page 206)
16 ounces (450 g) of shredded mozzarella or whole cheese curds

To make the gravy, splash the oil into a large pot over medium-high heat. Add the mushrooms and sauté, stirring frequently as they release their moisture. Continue cooking until the liquid simmers away and they're browned, 5 minutes or so. Add the onion and garlic and sauté until the vegetables are soft and aromatic, another 2 or 3 minutes. Add the lentils, water, wine, thyme, bay leaf, salt and pepper. Bring the gravy to a furious boil, then immediately reduce the heat to a slow, steady simmer. Cover tightly and cook until the lentils dissolve into thick gravy, about 45 minutes. Remove the bay leaf and thyme sprigs. For extra-smooth texture, purée the gravy using an immersion blender, blender or food processor.

To make the poutine, heap a batch of freshly cooked fries onto a plate or into a bowl. Sprinkle on a generous handful of shredded mozzarella, then top with a ladleful (or two!) of gravy.

Old-Fashioned Rice Pilaf with Thyme

There are many ways to cook rice. This basic method has stood the test of time because it's easy and delicious. First, simply stir rice grains in butter so they lightly brown and stay distinct. Then simmer the grains in seasoned broth so they absorb moisture *and* flavour. **SERVES 4**

2 tablespoons (30 mL) of butter

1 onion, minced

1 small carrot, grated

2 cloves of garlic, minced

1 cup (250 mL) of rice, rinsed

2 cups (500 mL) of real chicken broth or water

4 sprigs of fresh thyme

1 bay leaf

½ teaspoon (2 mL) of salt

Lots of freshly ground pepper

Melt the butter in a saucepot over medium heat. Add the onions, carrot and garlic and cook until soft and aromatic, 2 or 3 minutes. Add the rice and stir until the grains are evenly coated with butter and lightly toasted, another 2 or 3 minutes. Add the broth, thyme, bay leaf, salt and pepper. Bring to a furious boil, then immediately reduce the heat to a slow, steady simmer. Cover tightly and cook until all the liquid is absorbed and the rice is tender, about 15 minutes. Remove from the heat and rest, without uncovering, as the grains finish cooking, another 5 minutes or so. Remove the bay leaf and thyme stems and serve.

Wild Rice Sweet Potato Pilaf

Wild rice is an interesting alternative to run-of-the-mill everyday rice. It's just as easy to cook too, so it's a great way to add a tasty new ingredient to your repertoire. It's also Canadian! In this side dish its nutty flavour and chewy texture are complemented by the nutritional density and flavour of sweet potato. **SERVES 4 TO 6**

2 tablespoons (30 mL) of butter
1 onion, chopped
1 cup (250 mL) of wild rice
1 sweet potato, peeled and grated
2 cups (500 mL) of water or real chicken broth

1 bay leaf
1 teaspoon (5 mL) of salt
Lots of freshly ground pepper
The leaves and tender stems of 4 sprigs of fresh thyme, minced

Melt the butter in a medium saucepan over medium heat. Add the onions and cook until tender and fragrant, 2 to 3 minutes. Add the rice and stir until the grains are evenly coated with butter and lightly toasted, about 1 minute. (This will help them stay distinct as they cook.) Add the sweet potato, water, bay leaf, salt and pepper. Bring to a furious boil, then immediately reduce the heat to a slow, steady simmer. Cover and simmer until the rice is tender, 45 to 50 minutes. Remove from the heat and rest, without removing the lid, as the grain finishes absorbing the water, 5 minutes. Remove the bay leaf and stir in the thyme.

Tex-Mex Refried Beans with Bacon

Cooked and mashed beans are a staple on both sides of the Tex-Mex border, maybe because this is such an easy way to cook beans, or perhaps because it's just plain delicious. Either way, this a great dip hot or cold. You can roll burritos and layer quesadillas with it too. **SERVES 4**

4 thick slices of thick bacon, thinly sliced crosswise

1 onion, diced

1 red bell pepper, finely diced

4 cloves of garlic, minced

1 tablespoon (15 mL) of chili powder

1 tablespoon (15 mL) of ground oregano

1 teaspoon (5 mL) of ground cumin

2 cans (14 ounces/400 mL each) of pinto, kidney, red or black beans, drained and rinsed

½ cup (125 mL) of real chicken broth or water

1 teaspoon (5 mL) of Sriracha or your favourite hot sauce

Toss the bacon into a medium pot over medium-high heat. Add a big splash of water to help it cook evenly. Cook, stirring frequently, until the water has evaporated and the bacon is deliciously browned and evenly crispy, 10 minutes or so. Add a splash of water to help dissolve any browned bits of flavour adhering to the pan. Stir in the onions, red pepper, garlic, chili powder, oregano and cumin. Continue cooking until the vegetables soften, 10 minutes or so.

Stir in the beans, chicken broth and hot sauce. Continue simmering for another 5 minutes or so. Remove from the heat. With a potato masher, mash the beans as chunky or as smooth as you like.

Whole-Grain Stovetop Stuffing with Cranberries and Sage

This is a whole-grain version of the stuffing that anchors many a turkey feast. It's the perfect accompaniment for any dinner and can always be counted on to bring lots of familiar flavour to a festive table. **SERVES 8 TO 10**

For the grain pilaf
2 tablespoons (30 mL) of vegetable oil
1 large onion, chopped
2 stalks of celery, chopped
2 carrots, chopped
2 cloves of garlic, minced
1 cup (250 mL) of barley
1 cup (250 mL) of wild rice
2 cups (500 mL) of dried cranberries
2 cups (500 mL) of chopped walnuts

6 cups (1.5 L) of real chicken broth or water
2 sprigs of fresh thyme
1 bay leaf
½ teaspoon (2 mL) of salt
Lots of freshly ground pepper

To finish
4 green onions, thinly sliced
The leaves of 2 sprigs of fresh sage, finely chopped

Heat the oil in a large pot over medium-high heat. Toss in the onions, celery, carrot and garlic. Sauté until the vegetables are soft and aromatic, 2 or 3 minutes. Add the barley and wild rice and stir to lightly toast the grains and coat them with oil. Add the cranberries, walnuts, broth, thyme, bay leaf, salt and pepper. Bring to a furious boil, then immediately reduce the heat to a slow, steady simmer. Cover tightly and simmer until all the liquid is absorbed and the grains are tender, about 45 minutes. Remove from the heat and rest, without uncovering, as the grains finish cooking, 10 minutes or so. Remove the bay leaf and thyme sprigs.

To serve, stir in the green onions and sage.

Real Baking
and Real Treats

Real Bread

A loaf of homemade bread is a kitchen revelation. You can easily master this indispensable skill and impress yourself in your own home by keeping in mind just a few secrets: (1) For accuracy, weigh your ingredients. Measuring flour by volume can lead to inconsistent amounts. (2) Using all whole wheat dough will result in an unappetizingly heavy loaf, so incorporate some white flour to lighten the bread. (3) You don't have to laboriously knead the dough to develop gluten. Instead, use lots of water and be patient. With time, strong, elastic gluten will form all by itself.

MAKES 1 LOAF

16 ounces (500 g) of all-purpose flour

8 ounces (150 g) of whole wheat flour

4 ounces (100 g) of multigrain cereal mix or oatmeal flakes

2 teaspoons (0.3 ounces/10 g) of salt

A heaping ½ teaspoon (0.1 ounce/3 g) of instant yeast

19 ounces (550 g) of water

In a large bowl, whisk together the all-purpose flour, whole wheat flour, multigrain cereal, salt and yeast. Measure in the water, and with the handle of a wooden spoon, vigorously stir until a coarse dough forms. Continue stirring until all the flour is gathered up into an evenly mixed ball, a few minutes. Cover the bowl with plastic wrap and rest on your kitchen counter. In 8 hours or so, a strong, elastic dough will have formed and risen.

Preheat your oven to 425°F (220°C). Turn on your convection fan if you have one. Lightly oil a large loaf pan.

Gather the dough from the edge of the bowl, deflating it, and turn it out onto a lightly floured surface. Knead a few times, adding a little more flour if it sticks, and roll it into a tight ball. Transfer the dough to the loaf pan and encourage it into the corners. Rest, uncovered, until the dough has risen above the rim of the pan and doubled in size, an hour or two.

Bake until deliciously browned and crusty, 50 minutes or so. Rest until cool enough to handle, then remove the loaf from the pan and cool thoroughly on a wire rack before storing in a tightly sealed bag.

Ham and Cheddar Biscuits

Grating frozen butter into biscuit dough is one of the all-time great kitchen tricks. Adding cheddar and ham isn't bad either. Served with a salad or soup, these biscuits are hearty and delicious enough to anchor a meal. **MAKES 12 LARGE BISCUITS**

4 cups (1 L) of all-purpose flour

2 tablespoons (30 mL) of baking powder

½ teaspoon (2 mL) of salt

8 ounces (250 g) of butter, frozen

1 cup (250 mL) of diced ham

8 ounces (225 g) of cheddar, shredded

4 green onions, thinly sliced

1½ cups (375 mL) of milk

Preheat your oven to 400°F (200°C). Turn on your convection fan if you have one. Line a baking sheet with a silicone baking mat or parchment paper.

In a large bowl, whisk together the flour, baking powder and salt. Grate the butter through the large holes of a box grater into the flour below. Add the ham, cheddar and green onions, and working quickly with your fingers, toss the flour and butter shards together until everything is evenly distributed. Do not rub in the butter.

Pour in the milk and stir with the handle of a wooden spoon until a dough mass forms. (The handle of the spoon is gentler on the dough.) Working quickly, gently knead the dough in the bowl a few times until all the flour is gathered and absorbed. Knead and fold a few more times to maximize strength and flakiness.

Lightly flour your work surface. Turn out the dough and pat and roll it into a rectangle about 1 inch (2.5 cm) thick. Cut into 12 even pieces. Arrange the biscuits about 1 inch (2.5 cm) apart on the prepared baking sheet. Bake until they're crispy and golden brown, 20 to 25 minutes.

Whole Wheat Honey Cookies

These delicious cookies show off the nutty, wholesome flavour of whole wheat and the floral aromas of honey. They're a powerful reminder that the healthiest choices in our kitchen are often the tastiest. These are definitely a treat—not an everyday snack—but you'll be comforted knowing that you've baked them in your own oven! **MAKES 2 DOZEN COOKIES**

1 cup (250 mL) of buckwheat or your favourite honey
½ cup (125 mL) of butter, softened
1 egg
1 teaspoon (5 mL) of pure vanilla extract
2 cups (500 mL) of whole wheat flour

1 teaspoon (5 mL) of baking powder
½ teaspoon (2 mL) of nutmeg
¼ teaspoon (1 mL) of salt
2 cups (500 mL) of chopped walnuts, pecans, pumpkin seeds or sunflower seeds

Position racks in the middle and lower third of your oven and preheat the oven to 375°F (190°C). Turn on your convection fan if you have one. Line 2 cookie sheets with silicone baking mats or parchment paper.

Toss the honey and butter into the bowl of your stand mixer fitted with its paddle. Beat until smooth and creamy, scraping the sides of the bowl once or twice. Add the egg and vanilla and beat until smooth. In a separate bowl, whisk together the flour, baking powder, nutmeg and salt. Slowly add the dry ingredients to the egg mixture, beating until thoroughly combined. Stir in the nuts or seeds.

Using 2 spoons, drop the sticky dough by the spoonful onto the cookie sheets, leaving 3 inches (8 cm) or so between each cookie to allow for expansion. Bake until soft and golden brown, just 12 minutes or so. When the cookies are cool enough to handle, transfer them to wire racks to cool completely.

Apple Muffins

My mom has always loved to bake. Fortunately for my brothers and me, these muffins were one of her favourite recipes. You just can't beat the combination of apple and cinnamon. They always turned a simple breakfast into a special occasion. Bake a batch. I'm sure they'll impress your gang too! **MAKES 12 TO 16 MUFFINS**

1¼ cups (300 mL) of all-purpose flour
1 cup (250 mL) of whole wheat flour
1 cup (250 mL) of sugar
1 tablespoon (15 mL) of baking powder
2 teaspoons (10 mL) of cinnamon
½ teaspoon (2 mL) of salt

2 eggs
1 cup (250 mL) of milk
½ cup (125 mL) of butter, melted, or vegetable oil
2 teaspoons (10 mL) of pure vanilla extract
2 to 3 of your favourite apples
1 cup (250 mL) of walnut pieces

Position racks in the middle and lower third of your oven and preheat the oven to 400°F (200°C). Turn on your convection fan if you have one. Lightly oil 12 to 16 muffin cups (using 2 muffin pans if needed) with cooking spray or line with paper liners.

In a large bowl, whisk together the all-purpose flour, whole wheat flour, sugar, baking powder, cinnamon and salt. In a medium bowl, whisk together the eggs, milk, butter and vanilla. Grate the unpeeled apples directly into the wet ingredients, capturing any juice released. Add the liquid ingredients to the dry ingredients. Switch to a wooden spoon and with a few quick strokes, stir just until evenly combined.

Carefully spoon the batter into the muffin cups, filling each to the rim. Evenly sprinkle the walnut pieces over the top of each muffin. Bake until a toothpick poked into the centre comes out clean, 20 minutes or so. Turn out onto wire racks to cool.

Whole Wheat Cinnamon Rolls

These delicious rolls are made the old-fashioned way, with yeast, whole wheat flour and a secret ingredient: bananas. The dough takes advantage of the mashed ripe bananas' surprising ability to stand in for oil. Plus, they add sweetness and moisture to the rolls. There's no doubt that these are a treat, but every little bit of nutrition helps! **MAKES 12 ROLLS**

For the dough
1 cup (250 mL) of milk
½ cup (125 mL) of butter, cut into chunks
¼ cup (60 mL) of brown sugar
3 ½ cups (875 mL) of all-purpose flour
2 cups (500 mL) of whole wheat flour
1 package (2 ¼ teaspoons/11 mL) of instant yeast
¼ teaspoon (1 mL) of salt
2 very ripe bananas, mashed
1 egg, lightly beaten

For the filling
2 more very ripe bananas
½ cup (125 mL) of butter, softened
½ cup (125 mL) of brown sugar
2 tablespoons (30 mL) of cinnamon
1 tablespoon (15 mL) of pure vanilla extract

Make the dough. In a small saucepan, combine the milk, butter and brown sugar. Stirring constantly, heat just long enough for the butter to melt and the sugar to dissolve. Remove from the heat and cool for a few minutes.

In the bowl of your stand mixer, whisk together the all-purpose flour, whole wheat flour, yeast and salt. Attach your dough hook. Pour in the milk mixture and knead on low speed until all the ingredients come together. Add the bananas and egg, and continue to knead on low speed until the dough is smooth and elastic. Remove the dough hook, cover and rest at room temperature until the dough doubles in size, about 2 hours.

Meanwhile, make the filling. Combine the bananas, butter, brown sugar, cinnamon and vanilla in a small bowl and mash into a smooth paste. Reserve.

Lightly oil a 13- x 9-inch (3.5 L) baking pan. Lightly flour your work surface. Turn out the dough and roll into an even rectangle about 18 x 24 inches (45 x 60 cm), with a long edge closest to you. Spread the filling evenly over of the dough, leaving a 1-inch (2.5 cm) border at the far edge. Starting from the edge closest to you, roll up the dough, pulling and stretching it gently to keep the roll as tight as possible. Pinch the seam to seal it shut. Using a sharp knife or a piece of dental floss, cut the log into 12 even pieces. Nestle them cut side up in the prepared pan. Let the rolls rise a second time until they double in size and fill the pan, about 1 hour.

Meanwhile, preheat your oven to 350°F (180°C). Turn on your convection fan if you have one.

Bake the rolls until they're golden brown, about 45 minutes.

Village Feast Strawberry Shortcakes

Every year my eastern Prince Edward Island community hosts the Village Feast, an incredible fundraising steak dinner for 1000 guests. This is the dessert we love to serve. We schedule the event to coincide with ripe local strawberries so our shortcake is always a hit! **SERVES 12**

For the strawberry rhubarb compote

1 pound (450 g) of rhubarb, cut into 1-inch (2.5 cm) chunks

1 cup (250 mL) of sugar

½ cup (125 mL) of water

2 large baskets (about 3 pounds/1.4 kg) of fresh local strawberries, hulled and halved

For the biscuits

¼ cup (60 mL) or so of raw sugar

4 cups (1 L) of all-purpose flour

¼ cup (60 mL) of white sugar

2 tablespoons (30 mL) of baking powder

1 tablespoon (15 mL) of freshly grated nutmeg

¼ teaspoon (1 mL) of salt

2½ cups (625 mL) of whipping cream

1 teaspoon (5 mL) of pure vanilla extract

1 tablespoon (15 mL) of milk

For the whipped cream

2 cups (500 mL) of whipping cream

2 tablespoons (30 mL) of sugar

1 teaspoon (5 mL) of pure vanilla extract

Make the strawberry rhubarb compote. Toss the rhubarb, sugar and water into a medium pot. Bring to a furious boil over medium-high heat, then immediately reduce the heat to a slow, steady simmer. Cook until the rhubarb softens considerably to the point where it breaks down, 10 to 15 minutes. Cool completely, then stir in the strawberries.

Meanwhile, make the biscuits. Preheat your oven to 425°F (220°C). Turn on your convection fan if you have one. Line a baking sheet with a silicone baking mat or parchment paper. Place the raw sugar in a shallow dish and set aside.

In a large bowl, whisk together the flour, white sugar, baking powder, nutmeg and salt. Pour in the whipping cream and vanilla. Using the handle of a wooden spoon, vigorously stir until a coarse dough forms. Lightly flour your work surface. Turn out the dough and knead with conviction a few times until a firm dough forms. Pat the dough into an even disc about 1 inch (2.5 cm) thick. Cut into 12 even wedges. Lightly brush the tops with milk, then dip into the raw sugar, shaking off any excess. Transfer to the prepared baking sheet. Bake until golden brown, about 15 minutes. Cool on wire racks.

In a large bowl, whip the cream with the sugar and vanilla until thick, 3 to 5 minutes depending on how strong you are.

Build the shortcakes by cutting the biscuits open, layering the fruit and whipped cream on the bottom half, and topping with the other half.

Apple Tarts with Whole Wheat Crust

These tarts are just as delicious as an apple pie but much easier to make. Their delightful handmade appearance is a reminder to your guests that homemade always trumps store-bought! **MAKES 2 TARTS, EACH SERVING 6 TO 8**

For the crust
2 ½ cups (625 mL) of whole wheat flour
2 tablespoons (30 mL) of sugar
¼ teaspoon (1 mL) of salt
½ cup (125 mL) of butter, frozen
¾ cup (175 mL) of ice water

For the filling
2 pounds (900 g) or so of your favourite apples (6 to 8)
¼ cup (60 mL) of brown sugar
¼ cup (60 mL) of butter, cut into small pieces
2 tablespoons (30 mL) of whole wheat flour
1 tablespoon (15 mL) of cinnamon
1 tablespoon (15 mL) of pure vanilla extract
1 tablespoon (15 mL) of milk
1 teaspoon (5 mL) of coarse sugar

Make the crust. Whisk together the flour, sugar and salt in a large bowl. Grate the butter through the large holes of a box grater into the flour below. Working quickly, toss the flour and butter shards together with your fingers until they're evenly mixed. Do not rub in the butter. Pour in the water and stir with the handle of a wooden spoon until a coarse dough mass forms. Lightly flour your work surface. Turn out the dough and knead until all the flour is gathered up and a smooth dough forms. Divide into 2 even pieces, pat into discs and wrap with plastic wrap. Refrigerate until firm, an hour or so, even overnight.

Make the filling. Without peeling them, thinly slice the apples. In a large bowl, toss the apples with the brown sugar, butter, flour, cinnamon and vanilla.

Position racks in the middle and lower third of your oven and preheat the oven to 375°F (190°C). Turn on your convection fan if you have one. Line 2 baking sheets with silicone baking mats or parchment paper.

Make the tarts. Lightly flour your work surface. Roll one dough disc out into a circle about 14 inches (35 cm) in diameter. If the dough is too tough to roll or is cracking around the edges, let it warm at room temperature for a few minutes before continuing. To keep the dough from sticking, every time you double the surface area, dust again and flip over.

Loosely fold the dough into quarters, then carefully transfer to a prepared baking sheet before unfolding back into a circle. Pile half the apples in the middle, leaving a couple inches of border all the way around. Fold the overhanging dough over the apples, overlapping slightly and pleating the dough as necessary to frame the filling. Repeat with the other disc of dough and the remaining apples.

Lightly brush the dough edges with milk and sprinkle with coarse sugar. Bake until the crust is beautifully golden brown and the apples are tender, about 1 hour. Cool 15 minutes or so before cutting.

Chai-Spiced Banana Bread and Banana "Ice Cream"

Banana bread is the perfect way to show off the mysteriously aromatic flavours of a chai spice blend and an inventive "ice cream" of sorts. Next time you have a few extra ripe bananas, peel, slice and freeze them. You'll be poised to make a deliciously smooth and remarkably easy frozen topping that's indistinguishable from ice cream! **MAKES 1 LOAF AND ENOUGH ICE CREAM TO SERVE 8 TO 12**

For the banana "ice cream"
6 ripe bananas
1 tablespoon (15 mL) of honey
½ teaspoon (2 mL) of pure vanilla extract

For the banana bread
2 cups (500 mL) of all-purpose flour
2 teaspoons (10 mL) of cinnamon
1 teaspoon (5 mL) of ground ginger
1 teaspoon (5 mL) of ground cardamom
1 teaspoon (5 mL) of ground cloves

1 teaspoon (5 mL) of baking soda
¼ teaspoon (1 mL) of salt
¼ cup (60 mL) of pumpkin seeds
¼ cup (60 mL) of sunflower seeds
¼ cup (60 mL) of chia seeds
¼ cup (60 mL) of ground flaxseeds
2 eggs
¾ cup (175 mL) of brown sugar
4 very ripe bananas, mashed
½ cup (125 mL) of vegetable oil
1 tablespoon (15 mL) of pure vanilla extract

Freeze the bananas for the "ice cream" in advance. Peel and thinly slice them and spread them out on a baking sheet lined with a silicone baking mat or parchment paper. Freeze until solid, an hour or two, even overnight. Reserve in a resealable freezer bag until you need them.

Make the banana bread. Preheat your oven to 350°F (180°C). Turn on your convection fan if you have one. Lightly oil a loaf pan with cooking spray.

In a medium bowl, whisk together the flour, cinnamon, ginger, cardamom, cloves, baking soda and salt. In a small bowl, combine the pumpkin seeds, sunflower seeds, chia seeds and flaxseeds.

In the bowl of a stand mixer fitted with the paddle, beat the eggs and brown sugar until light and fluffy. Add the mashed bananas, oil and vanilla and continue to beat until evenly combined. Add the flour mixture and mix thoroughly. Gently stir in the seed mixture. Pour the batter into the prepared loaf pan. Bake until a skewer inserted in the centre eases out cleanly, 1 hour or so.

Make the banana "ice cream." Toss the frozen banana slices into your food processor. Process the bananas, scraping down the sides once or twice, until they transform into a smooth consistency like soft serve. Add the honey and vanilla and process just a few seconds more to mix in. Transfer to a container and reserve in the freezer. You can keep this for weeks.

Slice the banana bread into thick slices. Serve as is or, for even more flavour, pop into your toaster. Serve with a big scoop of fresh banana "ice cream."

Mocha Squares with Dark Chocolate Ganache

Chocolate plus coffee equals mocha. Chocolate plus cream equals decadence. Mocha cake plus ganache equals heaven. Enough math? Good thing you don't have to add up any more reasons to get baking! **MAKES 24 SQUARES**

For the ganache
8 ounces (225 g) of dark chocolate, chopped
2 cups (500 mL) of whipping cream

For the cake
2 cups (500 mL) of sugar
1 cup (250 mL) of all-purpose flour
¾ cup (175 mL) of whole wheat flour
¾ cup (175 mL) of cocoa powder
2 teaspoons (10 mL) of baking soda

¼ teaspoon (1 mL) of salt
2 eggs
1 cup (250 mL) of brewed coffee
1 cup (250 mL) of milk
½ cup (125 mL) of vegetable oil
1 tablespoon (15 mL) of pure vanilla extract

To finish
Your favourite nuts, seeds or other crunchy toppings

Make the ganache. Toss the chocolate into a heatproof bowl. In a small pot over medium heat, bring the cream to a bare simmer. Pour the cream over the chocolate and rest for 2 or 3 minutes. Gently stir until the chocolate is smoothly melted. Transfer to a large resealable plastic bag, squeeze out as much air as possible, and seal tightly. Refrigerate until you're ready to frost the cake.

Preheat your oven to 350°F (180°C). Turn on your convection fan if you have one. Lightly oil a 13- x 9-inch (3.5 L) cake pan with cooking spray, then line with parchment paper folded down one side, across the bottom and up the opposite edge, leaving some overhang.

Make and bake the cake. In a large bowl, whisk together the sugar, all-purpose flour, whole wheat flour, cocoa, baking soda and salt. In another bowl, whisk together the eggs, then whisk in the coffee, milk, vegetable oil and vanilla. Pour the wet mixture into the dry, switch to a wooden spoon and stir until smooth. Pour the batter into the cake pan and bake until a skewer inserted in the centre comes out clean, 35 minutes or so. Rest until firm, 10 minutes or so, then remove from the pan by lifting the two sides of the parchment paper. Rest on a wire rack until completely cool.

To decorate, carefully cut the cake into 24 portions. Snip one corner off the ganache bag and top each piece of cake with a thick swirl of ganache. Finish with a shower of your favourite nuts, seeds or other crunchy topping.

Hot Hot Cocoa with Vanilla Marshmallows

As you sip a steaming mug of this delicious hot cocoa, you'll notice a little bit of extra flavour, a touch of spicy heat to accent the warmth in your cup. Cayenne—a surprisingly delicious way to brighten the flavours of this simple indulgence. Of course a melting homemade marshmallow doesn't hurt either! You'll enjoy making a batch of your own. **SERVES 8, WITH LEFTOVER MARSHMALLOWS**

For the marshmallows
2 cups (500 mL) of water
3 cups (750 mL) of sugar
4 envelopes (¼ ounce/7 g each) of unflavoured gelatine
¼ teaspoon (1 mL) of salt
1 tablespoon (15 mL) of pure vanilla extract
½ cup (125 mL) of cocoa powder

For the hot cocoa
10 cups (2.5 L) of milk
2 tablespoons (30 mL) of pure vanilla extract
½ cup (125 mL) of cocoa powder
½ cup (125 mL) of brown sugar
2 teaspoons (10 mL) of ground allspice
¼ teaspoon (1 mL) of cayenne pepper

Make the marshmallows. Lightly oil an 8-inch (2 L) square cake pan with cooking spray. Measure 1¼ cups (300 mL) of the water into a small pot fitted with a candy thermometer. Carefully sprinkle the sugar into the water, taking care to avoid getting it on the sides of the pot. Without stirring, heat the works over medium-high heat. The hot water will dissolve the sugar into sugar syrup. Continue heating as the syrup rapidly boils and reaches 240°F (115°C), about 10 minutes.

Meanwhile, measure the remaining ¾ cup (175 mL) of water into the bowl of your stand mixer. Sprinkle the gelatine evenly over the water. Let the mixture stand, allowing the granules to rehydrate and swell, about 5 minutes.

Fit the mixer with the whisk attachment and stir the gelatine mixture on the lowest speed. Carefully pour in the hot sugar syrup, taking care to direct the flow away from the sides of the bowl directly into the gelatine. Add the salt. To cut down on splatter, cover the bowl loosely with a kitchen towel, then gradually increase the speed to the highest setting. Continue whipping until the mixture cools, stiffens and becomes thick and fluffy, about 15 minutes. Add the vanilla and whip just until thoroughly mixed. Pour the mixture into the prepared pan and use a spatula to smooth it into a thick, even layer. Cover and cool at room temperature until firm, an hour or two, even overnight.

Turn marshmallow out onto a cutting board and cut into 2-inch cubes. Sift the cocoa powder into a large bowl to break up any lumps. Toss the marshmallows in the cocoa a few at a time until they're lightly coated, dusting off excess. Store in a tightly sealed container.

Make the hot cocoa. Pour the milk and vanilla into a pot over medium-high heat. Whisk in the cocoa powder, brown sugar, allspice and cayenne and bring just to a simmer. Keep a close eye on the cocoa to keep it from bubbling over. Ladle into mugs and top with a marshmallow or two.

Homemade Staples

Beefy Broth

A good old-fashioned pot full of simmering beefy broth will infuse your home with tantalizing aromas and fill your table with incomparable richness. For best results take your time browning the meat. The deep caramelizing adds immeasurably to the broth's richness. It may seem wasteful to discard the meat and vegetables at the end, but after hours of simmering they're spent. **MAKES 8 TO 10 CUPS (2 TO 2.5 L)**

2 tablespoons (30 mL) of vegetable oil
2 pounds (900 g) or so of oxtails or beef shanks
A 5.5-ounce (156 mL) can of tomato paste
2 onions, coarsely chopped
2 carrots, coarsely chopped
2 stalks of celery, coarsely chopped

8 cups (2 L) of water
2 cups (500 mL) of red wine
1 bay leaf
1 teaspoon (5 mL) of salt
Lots of freshly ground pepper

Heat the oil in a large, heavy soup pot or Dutch oven over medium-high heat. Working in batches if necessary, brown the meat deeply and thoroughly on all sides. You may have to endure some smoke but it's a small price to pay for the rich, deep flavours that can only come from respectfully browned meat. Listen to the heat. A silent pan means nothing. A sizzle is the sound of flavour. Too loud, though, and a sizzling pan becomes a smoking-burning pan.

Return all the meat to the pot and add the tomato paste, onions, carrots, celery, water, wine, bay leaf, salt and pepper. Bring to a furious boil, then reduce the heat to a slow, steady simmer. Cover tightly and simmer gently, without stirring, as the browned flavours and aromatic vegetables infuse the broth with rich, meaty flavour, 3 to 4 hours.

Strain the broth. Reserve the beefy bits if you're making a stew or soup, and discard the bones and vegetables. If you have time, chill the broth in the fridge, then peel off the congealed layer of fat. To use the broth immediately, let it settle and then carefully ladle away as much of the fat as possible.

Nutmeg Ketchup

Commercial ketchup, though always flavoured with nutmeg, is generally quite one-dimensional and bland. This recipe goes much further. It's packed with aromatic personality, sunny tomato flavour and a delicious balance of sweet and sour. Just the thing to amp up your next round of cheeseburgers! **MAKES 5 CUPS (1.25 L) OR SO**

A 28-ounce (796 mL) can of diced tomatoes

A 5.5-ounce (156 mL) can of tomato paste

1 onion, diced

4 cloves of garlic, thinly sliced

2 bay leaves

1 cup (250 mL) of sugar

½ cup (125 mL) of brown sugar

½ cup (125 mL) of cider vinegar

½ cup (125 mL) of red wine vinegar

½ cup (125 mL) of extra-virgin olive oil

2 tablespoons (30 mL) of freshly grated nutmeg

½ teaspoon (2 mL) of ground allspice

½ teaspoon (2 mL) of salt

Lots of freshly ground pepper

Measure everything into a saucepan. Bring to a furious boil over medium-high heat, then immediately reduce the heat to a slow, steady simmer. Simmer, uncovered and stirring frequently, until the flavours concentrate and the mixture reduces by half, about an hour.

Remove from the heat, fish out the bay leaves and cool for a few minutes. Purée until smooth in your blender or food processor or in the pot with an immersion blender. Store tightly sealed, refrigerated, for up to a month or so.

Canadian Mustard

Canada grows more of the world's mustard seeds than any other country. This beautiful crop loves our climate and fills the prairies with yellow flowers. Yellow mustard seeds are only mildly spicy, so if you prefer real heat, use the much spicier brown seeds. **MAKES ABOUT 2 CUPS (500 ML)**

1 cup (250 mL) of yellow mustard seeds
1 cup (250 mL) of sweet apple cider
1 cup (250 mL) of cider vinegar

2 of your favourite apples, unpeeled, cored and chopped
¼ cup (60 mL) of honey
2 teaspoons (10 mL) of salt

In a medium pot, stir together the mustard seeds, apple cider and cider vinegar. Cover tightly and rest at room temperature overnight.

Add the apples, honey and salt. Bring to a simmer over medium heat and cook, stirring occasionally, until the apple is very tender, 15 minutes or so. Cool for a few minutes before transferring to your blender or food processor. If you prefer whole-grain style mustards, pulse for just a few moments. For a smoother result, carry on until completely puréed. Transfer to a clean jar, seal tightly and refrigerate. The mustard keeps indefinitely.

Chipotle BBQ Sauce

Most commercial barbecue sauces are loaded with sugar and artificial flavours. They pale in comparison to this brightly flavoured sauce. It has just enough spicy heat to get your attention but not so much that it overwhelms your palate. **MAKES 6 TO 7 CUPS (1.5 TO 1.75 L)**

A 28-ounce (796 mL) can of crushed tomatoes
A 5.5-ounce (156 mL) can of tomato paste
2 onions, chopped
1 red bell pepper, chopped
1 head of garlic, cloves chopped
2 to 3 chipotle peppers in adobo sauce, chopped

½ cup (125 mL) of molasses
½ cup (125 mL) of cider vinegar
¼ cup (60 mL) of your favourite mustard
2 tablespoons (30 mL) of chili powder
1 tablespoon (15 mL) of ground cumin
1 tablespoon (15 mL) of Worcestershire sauce

Measure all the ingredients into a large pot. Bring to a furious boil, then reduce the heat to a slow, steady simmer. Cover tightly and cook, stirring frequently, until the veggies are soft and tender, about 30 minutes. Remove from the heat and cool for a few minutes. Blend until smooth with an immersion blender, food processor or blender. Pour into clean jars and refrigerate or freeze until needed. The sauce keeps indefinitely.

Perpetual Crème Fraîche

Don't be fooled by the fancy French name—this is just old-fashioned sour cream at its best. This method is a fascinating reminder that fermentation is not only all around us but it can be a delicious path to rich flavour. You'll be blown away by the smooth creaminess and rich nuttiness that emerges after just a batch or two! **EACH BATCH MAKES 1 CUP (250 ML)**

For the starter batch
1 cup (250 mL) of whipping cream
2 tablespoons (30 mL) of buttermilk

For each subsequent batch
1 cup (250 mL) of whipping cream
2 tablespoons (30 mL) of the previous batch of crème fraîche

Make your starter batch. Simply stir together the whipping cream and buttermilk in a mason jar. Cover with a paper towel and secure it by screwing on the ring band. Rest undisturbed at room temperature in a warm place until the contents thicken noticeably like good sour cream, 24 hours or so. Enjoy immediately or replace the paper towel with the mason jar lid and refrigerate for 4 or 5 days.

When you're running low, make a new batch following the same procedure. In a clean mason jar, mix 1 cup (250 mL) of whipping cream with 2 tablespoons (30 mL) or so of your previous crème fraîche. Cover with paper towel, secure with a band and rest at room temperature until thickened. Refrigerate after that.

Preserved Lemon Purée

You can taste patience. After a month or so of being preserved in brine, the normal bitterness of lemons disappears and an intensely aromatic condiment emerges. It's a remarkable transformation and well worth the wait. **MAKES 2 CUPS (500 ML) OR SO**

6 organic lemons, scrubbed and dried
3 tablespoons (45 mL) of coarse sea salt

1 tablespoon (15 mL) of coriander seeds
1 bay leaf

Quarter 3 lemons lengthwise, stopping about ½ inch from the bottom so they stay intact. Working over a small bowl to catch any juices, gently spread each lemon open and remove as many seeds as you can. Sprinkle in a tablespoon (15 mL) or so of salt and some coriander seeds. Close the lemon back up, massaging the salt into the flesh and skin. Pack and squish the lemons into a standard 2-cup (500 mL) mason jar along with the bay leaf and any extra coriander seeds. Lemons vary in size, so if you can fit in a fourth, go for it.

Zest and juice the remaining 2 or 3 lemons into the small bowl and pour into the jar along with any accumulated salt. If the lemons are not submerged in juice, add more until they're covered. Screw the lid on tightly and give the jar a good shake. Refrigerate the lemons for 4 to 6 weeks, shaking and inverting the jar every few days.

After preserving, transfer the lemons and juice to your blender or food processor. Discard the bay leaf and any lemon seeds you come across. Purée until smooth. Transfer to a clean jar, tightly seal and refrigerate for up to a year.

Vanilla Rum Extract

Vanilla has the incredible ability to enhance the flavours around it without over-asserting itself. It's intensely aromatic, so a little bit goes a long way. Use this in place of store-bought vanilla extract. **MAKES 1 CUP (250 ML)**

12 plump, whole vanilla beans
1 cup (250 mL) of dark spiced rum

Slit the vanilla beans from tip to tip and split them open. Cut the beans into 1-inch (2.5 cm) lengths and place in a 1-cup (250 mL) mason jar. Pour in the rum and seal tightly. Shake gently and store at room temperature away from the sunlight. Shake every few days and patiently wait as the vanilla's floral aromas emerge and strengthen. In 6 to 8 weeks you'll be rewarded with your very own homemade batch of vanilla extract. Store at room temperature with the bean pieces still in the liquid.

Cinnamon Applesauce

One of my family's favourite fall traditions is wandering up and down the rows of trees at our local apple orchard, picking and tasting to our hearts' content, then heading home to make our winter's applesauce. We find that the best sauce is always made from a blend of ripe apples, and we love reminiscing every time we enjoy a bowl. **MAKES 8 CUPS (2 L) OR SO**

10 pounds (5 kg) or so of your favourite local apples
1 cup (250 mL) of brown sugar

1 cup (250 mL) of apple juice or water
2 tablespoons (30 mL) of cinnamon

Without peeling them, core the apples, cut into large chunks and toss into a large pot. Add the brown sugar, apple juice and cinnamon and stir to evenly distribute. Bring the works to a slow, steady simmer over medium heat. Cover tightly and cook, stirring frequently, until the apples soften and dissolve, 20 minutes or so. Pass the apples through a food mill or purée in a food processor. Refrigerate for up to a week or two or freeze for up to 6 months or so.

Cranberry Ginger Chutney

A memorable chutney always balances the sweetness of preserved fruit with a bit of bitterness, sourness, spice and fragrant aromas. This delicious condiment doesn't disappoint and will add lots of festive pizzazz to your holiday table. **MAKES 4 CUPS (1 L)**

A 12-ounce (340 g) package of fresh cranberries

2 of your favourite apples, peeled, cored and finely diced

1 onion, finely diced

A 2-inch (5 cm) knob of frozen ginger, finely grated

½ cup (125 mL) of dried apricots, chopped

½ cup (125 mL) of golden raisins

¼ cup (60 mL) of honey

¼ cup (60 mL) of cider vinegar

2 cloves of garlic, finely minced

½ teaspoon (2 mL) of red chili flakes

½ teaspoon (2 mL) of coriander or fennel seeds

Combine everything in a saucepan. Bring to a furious boil, then reduce the heat to a slow, steady simmer. Cook, uncovered and stirring frequently, just until the cranberries burst, about 20 minutes.

Bottle and refrigerate for up to a month or freeze for up to 6 months.

Strawberry Rhubarb Ginger Compote

When our local strawberries are in season we love to save as many as we can this way, so we can enjoy their fruity goodness all year long. We constantly find ourselves spooning this deliciousness over yogurt, ice cream, slices of cake or sweet biscuits with whipped cream for a shortcake treat!

MAKES 4 CUPS (1 L) OR SO

2 or 3 cups (500 mL) of thickly sliced rhubarb

1 cup (250 mL) of sugar

The zest and juice of 2 lemons

A 2-inch (5 cm) knob of frozen ginger, grated

3 or 4 cups (750 mL) of strawberries, hulled and halved

Toss the rhubarb, sugar, lemon zest, lemon juice and ginger into a medium pot. Bring to a furious boil over medium-high heat, then reduce the heat to a slow, steady simmer. Cook, stirring frequently, until the rhubarb softens and breaks down, 5 minutes or so. Stir in the strawberries, turn up the heat and continue cooking just long enough to heat them through, just another minute or two. Transfer to jars, seal tightly and refrigerate for a week or two or freeze in plastic totes.

Special Thanks

My family, team and I treasure the time we spent with this and all my books. We truly enjoy collaborating to create a viable resource for you that delivers on the title's promise. We understand the very real need for a trusted voice and a reliable source of inspiration. We strive to be accurate and relevant, to challenge and teach you as you cook. We believe in you, that you can achieve miracles in the kitchen if you try. We want you to succeed, and we work very hard to ensure you do.

Thank you for inspiring us to be our best so you can be yours.

Michael. Chazz. Gabe. Ariella. Camille. Tiffany. Maureen. Edna. Shannon. Shyla.

Index